Chaplain S.L. Bochonok

CHOOSING A PASTOR

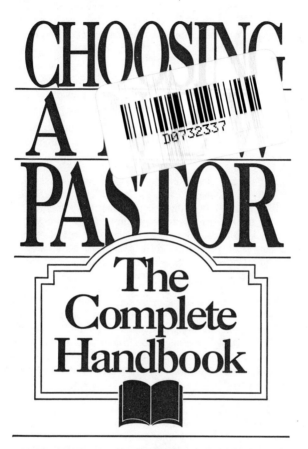

The Complete Handbook

HENRY A. VIRKLER, PH.D.

OLIVER NELSON

A Division of Thomas Nelson Publishers
Nashville, Tennessee

Published in Nashville, Tennessee, by Oliver-Nelson Books, a division of Thomas Nelson, Inc., Publishers, and distributed in Canada by Lawson Falle, Ltd., Cambridge, Ontario.

Unless otherwise noted, the Bible version used in this publication is the HOLY BIBLE: NEW INTERNATIONAL VERSION. Copyright © 1973, 1978, 1984 by the International Bible Society. Used by permission of Zondervan Bible Publishers. "A Case of Unprofessional Conduct," Jean Shaw, *Eternity,* February 1980. Reprinted by permission of *Eternity,* copyright © 1980, Evangelical Ministries, Inc., 1716 Spruce Street, Philadelphia PA 19103. "Clergy on Welfare," *Eternity,* September 1980. Reprinted by permission of *Eternity,* copyright © 1980, Evangelical Ministries, Inc., 1716 Spruce Street, Philadelphia PA 19103. "The Care and Feeding of Shepherds," Cliff Stabler, *Christianity Today,* n.d. Copyrighted and reprinted by permission of *Christianity Today.* Ideas and formulas for deriving fair salary structures for pastors are from copyrighted pamphlets written and published by Harold Sedrel over the last twenty years. Used by permission. Excerpts from *Critical Moment of Ministry,* Loren Mead. Used by permission from The Alban Institute, Inc., 4125 Nebraska Avenue, NW, Washington, D.C. 20016. Copyright 1986. All rights reserved. Excerpts from *Pastoral Transitions: From Endings to New Beginnings* (pages 27–29 and 66–67), Wm. Bud Phillips. Reprinted by permission from the Alban Institute, Inc., 4125 Nebraska Avenue, NW, Washington, D.C. 20016. Copyright 1988. All rights reserved. Excerpts from an unpublished paper on Questions Candidating Pastors Should Ask Pastoral Search Committees. Written by Rev. Dennis B. Lacy, n.d. Used with permission.

Library of Congress Cataloging-in-Publication Data

Virkler, Henry A.
    Choosing a new pastor : the complete handbook / Henry A. Virkler.
        p.   cm.
    Includes bibliographical references and index.
    ISBN 0-8407-9129-1
    1. Clergy—Appointment, call, and election. I. Title.
BV664.V57   1992
254—dc20   91–45559
                                                                        CIP

Printed in the United States of America.
1 2 3 4 5 6 — 97 96 95 94 93 92

To

DENNIS B. LACY

an excellent pastor and a cherished friend

Wanted—A rector for St. James' Church, He must possess all Christian graces and a few worldly ones; must have such tact and disposition as will enable him to side with all parties in the parish on all points, giving offense to none; should possess a will of his own, but agree with all the vestry; must be socially inclined and of dignified manners—affable to all, neither running after the wealthy nor turning his back upon the poor; a man of high-low church tendencies preferred. Must be willing to preach first-class sermons and do first-class work at second-class compensation—salary should not be so much of an object as the desire to be a zealous laborer in the vineyard; should be able to convince all that they are miserable sinners without giving offense. Each sermon must be short, but complete in itself—full of old-fashioned theology in modern dress— deep but polished, and free from the eloquence peculiar to newly-graduated theologians; should be young enough to be enthusiastic, but possess judgment of one of ripe years and experience. Only he who possesses the above qualifications need apply. To such a one will be given steady employment for a term of years.

—Milwaukee Sentinel, *June 16, 1875*

CONTENTS

Introduction

In many churches the congregation is responsible for, or has a significant role to play in, selecting and calling its own pastor. This book is primarily intended for people who serve on the board or pastor nominating committees of those churches. These include Baptist churches, Assemblies of God, Church of the Nazarene, Christian and Missionary Alliance churches, the Christian Church, some Lutheran synods, Churches of Christ, most independent churches, United Churches of Christ, Episcopal and Presbyterian churches.

In some of these denominations, particularly the last three listed, denominational staff have developed pastoral search guidelines. These guidelines are excellent and address, in abbreviated form, many suggestions included in this book. For members of such denominations this book can increase awareness of how other denominations do things and can give the rationale behind suggested procedures. It also can give the pros and cons of one approach or another.

This book will have the most value in the first several denominations listed above. In these denominations there often are no developed set of guidelines regarding pastoral searches, or the guidelines may still be in their formative state. Some of these denominations have two- or three-page outlines in their denominational handbooks. This book can help pastor nominating committees understand the purpose of the various steps in those outlines. (Why, for example, is it so important to do a self-study as part of the process of pastoral selection?) It will describe the many details involved in the complex task of identifying potential candidates, deciding which candidate is best for their church, and extending an invitation to him.

The Importance of Pastoral Longevity

In interviewing pastors, interim pastors, and denominational leaders from several denominations, I discovered a consensus about this point: they all view longer pastorates as healthier for everyone involved—for pastors, their families, and the church congregation. Long pastorates result when there is a good match between a pastor and a congregation.

Conversely, poor matches between pastors and congregations result in short pastorates, often ending in involuntary terminations, and are very hurtful to everyone involved. The pastor, his children, his spouse, the congregation's children, the congregation's adults—all suffer pain when a congregation fires a pastor because of a poor fit between him and the congregation. This book is an attempt to help churches make better selection decisions and reduce this source of pain.

The plan proposed in the following chapters integrates the recommendations from pastors and denominational leaders in several denominations, the recommendations from pastoral selection experts at the Alban Institute, and the recommendations from leadership selection experts in the fields of industrial psychology and organizational development. This plan has several goals:

1. It attempts to minimize the cost to the local congregation.

2. It attempts to minimize the time needed by the pastor nominating committee members, who usually have many other responsibilities besides their work on the committee.

3. It attempts to develop a procedure that doesn't result in many candidates who preach before the congregation in seemingly endless succession.

4. It attempts to help a congregation find a pastor who matches its needs within three to twelve months.

5. It attempts to develop a procedure that can be easily modified to meet the needs of a specific congregation or denomination.

Readers may note that I consistently use the pronoun *he* when referring to a pastor or pastoral candidate. By so doing, I am not attempting to take a stand on the issue of whether women should be involved in full-time pastoral ministries. Other books have examined that issue carefully. Individuals and committees must make a decision about it based on the evidence presented in Scripture, other books on the subject, and their thinking. I base my decision to use *he* when referring to pastors on two factors: (1) most pastors continue to be males, and (2) writing out *he* and *she* and *him* and *her* in all the places it should be done makes some sentences terribly convoluted and difficult to read. Please feel free to substitute the words *or she* as you read if this represents your theological understanding.

I would like to add a note about this book's subtitle. The words *The Complete Handbook* are not intended to claim that it possesses some sort of exclusive or final status. We are constantly learning more about the process of pastoral change, pastoral selection, and the emotional process a congregation goes through in grieving the loss of one pastor and accepting a new one. In that sense no human book will ever be *the* complete treatment of this or any other topic.

In this book I have attempted to gather the best ideas from many sources—books, pamphlets, pastors, and denominational leaders—and integrate them into one practical model. For that reason I hope it will provide a comprehensive guide for those church committees entrusted with the critical task of finding a new pastor for their congregation.

Acknowledgments

I would like to thank the following people for their willingness to be interviewed and to share ideas and materials that they have developed.

Rev. Bill Adams, Executive Presbyter, the Presbyterian Center (U.S.A.), Atlanta, Georgia.

Dr. Leslie M. Addison, State Superintendent, Assemblies of God, Macon, Georgia.

Dr. Richard Bush, Pastor, Grace Fellowship Alliance Church, Norcross, Georgia.

Rev. T. Daniel Casey, Pastor, Atlanta First Church of the Nazarene, Decatur, Georgia.

Dr. Tom Champness, Pastor, Redeemer Orthodox Presbyterian Church, Doraville, Georgia.

Rev. Jerry Copeland, District Superintendent, Christian and Missionary Alliance Church, Charlotte, North Carolina.

Dr. James Donovan, President, Atlanta Christian College, Atlanta, Georgia.

Rev. Joe Ford, Interim Pastor (Southern Baptist), Lilburn, Georgia.

Dr. G. Ross Freeman, Editor, Wesleyan Christian *Advocate,* Southeastern Jurisdictional Council on Ministries of the United Methodist Church, Atlanta, Georgia.

Rev. John Guse, Pastor and District President of the Wisconsin Synod Lutheran Church, Marietta, Georgia.

Rev. Daniel W. Hampton, Evangelism and Home Missions Director, North Georgia Churches of God, Doraville, Georgia.

Rev. Fred Hartley, Pastor, Lilburn Alliance Church, Lilburn, Georgia.

Rev. Clayton Hayes, Pastor, Christ Community Church, Clarkston, Georgia.

Rev. Sid Hopkins, Executive Director, Gwinnett Metro Baptist Association, Lawrenceville, Georgia.

Caroline Hughes, Canon of Education, Diocese of Atlanta (Episcopal Church), Atlanta, Georgia.

Rev. Dennis B. Lacy, Pastor, Calvary Assembly of God, Dunwoody, Georgia.

Rev. David McKee, Interim Pastor, Westminster Presbyterian Church, Snellville, Georgia.

Rev. Sandy Mullins, Assistant Conference Minister, Southeast Conference of the United Church of Christ, Decatur, Georgia.

Rev. Howard Porter, Office Manager, Georgia District Church of the Nazarene, Marietta, Georgia.

Rev. Danny Shoemake, Pastor, Stone Mountain Christian Church, Stone Mountain, Georgia.

John Vieths, Vicar, Sola Fide Lutheran Church, Lawrenceville, Georgia.

Dr. Ron Warren, Assistant to the Bishop, Southeastern Synod of the Evangelical Lutheran Church in America, Atlanta, Georgia.

Rev. Randall Williamson, Assistant to the Bishop, the United Methodist Center, Atlanta, Georgia.

Various Ways Churches Choose New Pastors

This first chapter includes three sections. The first identifies six significant differences between denominations as they select new pastors. The second organizes the various approaches into four broad categories and discusses how several denominations in these four categories go through the selection process. The third section discusses the important questions: Is there a theological basis for the way that we undertake the pastoral selection process? Is there more than one right way? Does God have one best person identified for each pastoral vacancy with our responsibility being to find that one person?

Significant Differences in the Pastoral Selection Process

Important Terms

Before beginning our discussion, it will be helpful to define two terms that will be used repeatedly in this book. A denomination's *polity* is its form of government. Baptist churches have one form of polity; Presbyterians have another.

A second important term is the *judicatory,* which is a generic name for a denomination's regional office and leadership. A presbytery is the name of the Presbyterian Church's judicatory; the presbytery for an area is composed of all the ministers in that area and one or more elders from each church in the area. According to Presbyterian polity, individual congregations are under the authority of their regional presbytery.

A diocese is the name of the judicatory of the Episcopal Church; individual churches within the diocese are under the authority of a regional bishop. An association is the name of the judicatory of Southern Baptist churches; according to Southern Baptist polity, each local congregation is autonomous—association officials have only an advisory capacity to local churches.

Six Important Differences

The most obvious difference between denominations in the pastoral selection process is that some denominations use an "appointive" process and others use a "calling" process. The United Methodist Church, the Roman Catholic Church, the Church of God, and the Armed Services use an appointive process; most other Protestant denominations use a calling process.

A second obvious difference is that in some denominations each congregation has local autonomy and in "connectional" denominations local churches are accountable to a higher denominational authority or group. Baptist churches, Assemblies of God, the Christian Church, and the Church of Christ have locally autonomous congregations. Episcopalians, Presbyterians, and Lutherans are connectional denominations.

Because of external differences in these processes, Christians have sometimes assumed that they have little to learn from and little helpful to share with members of other groups. I hope these next three chapters will show just how much we can learn from one another.

Besides these two differences, there are at least four others between denominations. Third, when choosing a new pastor, some denominations and congregations rarely take time to reflect on their past. As a result they may repeat the problems with a new pastor that they have had with former pastors. Other congregations and denominations do not feel they have done an adequate job of preparing for a new pastor if they have not looked carefully at their past (particularly if there were problems between the pastor and the congregation) and have come to an understanding of how and why those problems developed.

Fourth, some congregations and denominations rarely look below the surface-level tasks that need to be done (i.e., "get a new preacher"). Others use this time to carefully examine their mission and identity and frequently change them because of their examination. For example, a downtown church in a large city found that it had been losing membership for the last four years. The church had largely blamed this decrease on the former pastor. During the self-study, the committee realized that the population within a five-mile radius of the church had substantially changed over the last ten years. Yet, the church was still aiming its programs at the population that had lived in proximity to the church a decade earlier. The committee had to ask some basic questions: Should the church move to a location where its programs would reach the current members, or should it develop some new approaches that would have a greater attraction for the city residents who now lived close to it? Clearly the members of the congregation needed to decide this fundamental question before they could specify what kind of pastor they were looking for. Failure to do a careful self-study meant that they would probably pick a pastor oriented to the kinds of programs they had used for the last two decades. In a few years they would conclude that this pastor had also been ineffective in halting the church's losses.

A fifth difference is that some denominations have never heard of interim or vacancy consultants whereas other churches use them regularly. (Interim or vacancy consultants are people with special training who help a congregation objectively look at its history, identity, sense of mission, and expectations of the pastor. They also help the congregation and board make those changes that seem in the church's, and future pastor's, best interests.) Presbyterian and Episcopalian churches frequently call on interim consultants. Laypersons in many other Protestant denominations are not aware that interim consultants even exist.

Sixth, denominations pay varying amounts of attention to the emotional components of losing a pastor and accepting a new one. Some denominations attend to this issue hardly at all; other denominations and congregations believe it is important to realize that the loss of a pastor often affects people at a deep emotional level. They believe that a pastor often comes to represent something like a spiritual father to many congregational members, though these people may not always be consciously aware of this perception. Loss of this person initiates a grieving process. If individuals and congregations do not express this grief in healthy ways, it may be buried and come out in not-so-healthy ways.

A similar situation can occur when a pastor leaves under pressure. Such departures can be caused by unfulfilled expectations of the church and the pastor, by antagonistic actions of a few members, or by mistakes of a pastor or his spouse. There are likely to be a whole gamut of conflicting emotions in the hearts of the congregation. Denominational leaders, interim pastors, and pastors agreed that if the congregation does not have some healthy way of expressing and working through these feelings, they are likely to be expressed in various oblique ways during the next pastorate. Often the next pastor has a short, frequently painful tenure as church members unconsciously transfer unresolved feelings onto him.

These same church leaders were in agreement about another point. Like a dysfunctional family, a church family often tries to deny the existence of any problems. Church members may feel uncomfortable with the vulnerability that comes from admitting problems. They may fear that admitting problems will scare off any potential pastor who is considering them. Such congregations are not a minority. Denominational leaders said that most congregations tend to deny their

4

emotions—whether of grief, anger, hurt, or anxiety—when a pastor leaves. However, several churches, church consulting groups (e.g., the Alban Institute), and denominations are beginning to try to help congregations work through the emotional unfinished business that they sometimes have after a pastor leaves.* We'll discuss some of that work in chapter 3.

Four Broad Approaches for Selecting a New Pastor

Pastors may be chosen and maintained in that role in one of four ways:

1. Appointment by the judicatory; connectional oversight by the judicatory.

2. Preselection of a group of candidates by the judicatory, choice of one of the candidates by a congregation, connectional oversight by the judicatory.

3. Selection of a candidate by a congregation, approval by the judicatory, connectional oversight by the judicatory.

4. Congregational selection; congregational autonomy (no congregational oversight by the judicatory).

Each of these methods and examples of some denominations that use them will be described below. Be aware that regional and individual variations in methods occur throughout the United States.

Appointment by the Judicatory; Connectional Oversight by the Judicatory

Examples of this approach include the United Methodist Church and the Church of God (the Pentecostal denomination

---

Unfinished business refers to a psychological phenomenon: persons who have strong unexpressed emotional feelings are unable to deal objectively and fairly with other tasks and people in their lives because the unexpressed feelings keep intruding into their present work and relationships.

headquartered in Cleveland, Tennessee). This appointment is not a unilateral process. In both denominations the local congregation, or its elected representatives, has input in the appointment process.

The United Methodist Church

Each church within the Methodist system develops a church profile that includes a statement of its needs, its characteristics, and its mission. Each pastor, with his district superintendent, develops a personal profile that identifies his gifts, professional experience and expectations, and the needs and concerns of his spouse and family. Churches and pastors update their profiles annually.

In January every year each pastor and his parish committee reflect on how the church is realizing its potential. A request for a change in appointment can be initiated by a pastor, his parish committee, his district superintendent, or his bishop.

From these requests the bishop makes up a "move list," using the profiles to match pastors' needs and gifts with churches needing complementary talents. He consults with his cabinet (composed of the bishop and district superintendents), reviewing possible placements for specific pastors, and receives feedback from them. In addition he asks those pastors wishing to move to rank their preferences of the churches that are expected to have a vacancy. He continues this process until each pastor has an appointment and each church has a pastor. The district superintendent checks out potential appointments with individual pastors and with the parish committee of each church. He also shares with them the basis for the change and the process used in making the appointment. Sometimes during this consultation the bishop and his cabinet recognize that a certain appointment should not be made. They then repeat the process, considering the new information, and the bishop makes a new appointment. The bishop or district superintendent privately informs the pastor and parish committee of the final appointment decisions, and in June of each year the new appointments are publicly announced.

Connectional oversight by the judicatory means that each congregation may not hire or fire its pastor. The denomination, through the person of the bishop and his cabinet, is connected to, and has authority over, individual congregations and pastors.

Each district superintendent usually has fifty to sixty pastors and churches under his care. If conflict arises between a pastor and his parish committee, the bishop, district superintendent, or someone else working with the church and pastor tries to resolve the conflict. All effort to resolve a problem is first exhausted before pastors are moved. There is a strong belief that moving doesn't resolve problems. When a conflict occurs, the denomination has a Conference Council on Ministries composed of skilled persons who go into churches, listen to all parties, and offer suggestions. Pastoral counselors are also available to provide personal counseling and consultation. It was estimated that United Methodist pastors remain an average of four years with each congregation, with some pastors staying as long as twenty-five years.*

The Church of God

The Church of God has a similar system, although pastors do not move based on the annual calendar. If a pastor desires to move, he submits his name confidentially to the state overseer. Churches also may request a pastoral change. The state overseer, in consultation with the district overseer, prays and studies those pastors and churches wishing to make a change. The overseers recommend the name of a pastor willing to move whose talents and background appear to best fit the needs of a church. If the church is uncomfortable with the first recommendation, the state and district overseers will meet again and will recommend a second candidate.

As in other connectional denominations, the local congrega-

---

*None of the denominational officials were able to give statistically derived data on the average length of stay of pastors in their denominations, so these figures should be viewed as estimates only.

tion does not have the authority to hire or fire a pastor. The pastor "belongs" to the denomination—he is not considered an employee of a local church.

The state and district overseers monitor the statistics of every church monthly. If they see a continuing decline, or if the pastor or congregation requests it, they will meet with the pastor and congregation to discuss the situation. Some pastors of connectional denominations (other than the Church of God) said that when there is a conflict between the pastor and the congregation, they perceive that their judicatory will always recommend that the pastor leave rather than face the possibility of a church split or church decline if the denomination retains the pastor in that congregation. The Church of God appears to be different in this regard. If the church overseers believe the problem lies with the congregation rather than with the pastor, they will support the pastor, even if that results in a temporary decline in the size of the particular congregation. The average stay of a Church of God pastor with a given congregation was estimated to be between five and eight years.

Preselection of a Group of Candidates by the Judicatory, Choice of One of the Candidates by a Congregation, Connectional Oversight by the Judicatory

Denominations that use this approach include the Christian and Missionary Alliance, the Lutheran Church, and the Church of the Nazarene. The denomination's judicatory prescreens applicants for pastoral vacancies, and the judicatory forwards names of those approved during this prescreening to the local congregation. The local church chooses one of those candidates to be its pastor.

The Christian and Missionary Alliance

In the Christian and Missionary Alliance, the process usually begins when a pastor decides to make a move or announces his resignation to the governing board and the district superintendent. (The district superintendent is equivalent to the bishop in the United Methodist judicatory.)

The district superintendent prescreens a list of candidates that he believes would match the needs of the particular congregation. His prescreening includes a credential review (review of education, resume, and ordination or licensing) and a review of a pastor's references (has he served effectively in other churches? what does his current district superintendent say about him?). The district superintendent has resumes of pastors who have initiated contact with him. He also may contact a pastor the congregation has requested to see if he is willing to be considered for a move. He may contact a pastor he believes would be well-suited to that particular church. He prescreens a person requested by the congregation in the same manner he screens all other candidates. Sometimes he will not approve a person the congregation has requested if he believes the person is not an appropriate candidate.

The governing board of each congregation has some latitude in how to decide among the recommended candidates. All congregations invite a candidate to spend a weekend with them. The congregation may then be asked to participate in a "straw vote." This congregational vote is not a call. The governing board of the church is empowered to make the decision to call or not to call, although most boards consider the straw vote in making their decision. The decision by the governing board needs to be affirmed by the district superintendent to be binding.

The average length of a pastor with one congregation within the Christian and Missionary Alliance was estimated to be four years. The Christian and Missionary Alliance is connectional; a local congregation cannot fire a pastor. If conflict arises, the elders and the pastor first attempt to work this out themselves. If this fails, the district superintendent may come to the church to help them resolve it. He will work with the pastor and the governing board to help both sides see how they may be contributing to the problem. If the pastor has significant problems, the district superintendent can recommend or require counseling. If he believes the church is contributing significantly to the problems, he can appoint an interim pastor or pastor with a specific assignment to work on certain problems with the congregation.

The Lutheran Church: Wisconsin Synod

The Wisconsin Synod of the Lutheran Church is particularly interesting because its process *prohibits* the potential pastor and the congregation from meeting each other during the pastoral selection process. A meeting between the candidate and the congregation is considered crucial to the selection process by most denominations, and yet Wisconsin Synod Lutherans have developed a system that seems to work well without it.

When there is a pastoral vacancy, the congregation contacts the district president (the same as bishop in other polities). The members may hold a pre-call meeting with him to talk about what the church needs and wants. The district president then carefully reviews his information about available pastors.

Each district president has extensive information on the available pastors in his synod, including information from their seminary days, their pastoral intern work, and their present work. Because it is a small synod, one or more of the district presidents are likely to know each pastor well, and district presidents consult with one another often in this process. Because of the high degree of trust between district presidents, they are often willing to share important information with one another that they might not share with a committee.

The district president produces a "call list," which is a list of candidates he recommends to the church, including a one- to two-paragraph biographical sketch on each. He usually will supply the congregation with a list of three or four names. The congregation may request a particular name. If the district president believes the man has the gifts to serve in that congregation, he may add the suggested name to the list.

The local congregation prays about God's leading, then extends a call to one person on that list, with a description of the church, its current ministries, and its community. The called pastor, after a time of prayer, responds with an answer. If he does not accept the call, the church prays and calls another candidate in a similar fashion until someone accepts.

Two things are unique in this process of selection. First, there is a strong emphasis on the providence of God working through the process (for example, the congregation and the pastoral candidate do not believe a personal meeting is necessary because God will work in the hearts of the congregation and the potential pastor to confirm His will). Second, the congregations place a very high level of trust in their district presidents, believing that the candidates they recommend have been carefully screened and that, therefore, it is unnecessary for them to meet the pastor before calling him.

Within the Wisconsin Synod a congregation cannot fire a pastor. If a conflict develops between a pastor and his congregation, the district president usually designates a circuit pastor for that church. The circuit pastor attempts to provide counsel and advice in the situation (each circuit pastor has seven to ten churches under his care). If the circuit pastor cannot find a way of resolving the problem, he refers the matter back to the district president. The pastor cannot be removed by the congregation except for teaching false doctrine, being immoral, or failing to live up to the qualifications of 1 Timothy 3. This synod believes that the Lord, not the congregation, should move a pastor. Most pastoral changes occur because a pastor accepts a call to another church or because he realizes that his ministry to a particular congregation has ended and resigns. The average length of stay per pastorate was estimated to be seven years.

Selection of a Candidate by a Congregation, Approval by the Judicatory, Connectional Oversight by the Judicatory

This process is the reverse order of the last one. Here the pastor nominating committee first selects and then the judicatory approves rather than the judicatory preselecting and the congregation choosing. A pastor nominating committee identifies one or more candidates, but the individual must be approved by the judicatory before the call can be made.

The relationship is a three-sided one that includes the pastor, the congregation, and the judicatory. As in other connectional approaches, the judicatory can become reinvolved if problems develop between pastor and congregation. The congregation cannot fire a pastor. Examples include the Episcopalian and Presbyterian denominations.

The Episcopal Church

Each Episcopal church has a vestry (the counterpart to a parish committee in the United Methodist Church or a deacon board in a Baptist church). Pastors in Episcopal churches are called rectors. The pastoral search process begins when a rector and a vestry call the bishop of their diocese to tell him that the rector will be leaving.

The search process will differ from one diocese (regional area) to another, but in general Episcopal churches use the following procedure. The bishop or one of his canons (assistants) meets with the vestry and goes over the recommended search process. At this point the vestry appoints a search committee and gives them their charge.

The diocese may have trained search consultants who will help the search committee as needed. The first step for the search committee is to develop a parish profile (a specific description of the kind of person they are looking for). They then develop ways of identifying possible candidates. Within the Episcopal Church this usually includes a computerized search through the National Church Office in New York, which matches parishes with names of candidates nationwide. The search committee also may receive leads through their bishop and his staff and through personal relationships.

After gathering names and basic ministerial information about these potential candidates, the search committee devises some way to make initial decisions. Committee members then begin to go out in teams to talk with the most likely candidates. After these interviews, the committee makes further decisions. Another round of team visits may follow.

The vestry will interview one or more candidates submitted to them by the search committee. When they have settled on one, they will submit this person's name to the bishop for his approval. After the bishop has given his approval, the vestry will extend a call to the pastor.

An Episcopal bishop doesn't move rectors. Usually, a rector and the vestry have to agree before there is a pastoral move. If a rector and his vestry disagree about some issue, the diocese encourages them to work through this conflict themselves if possible. If that is not possible, the diocese sometimes uses a consultant to try to bring about agreement. If the situation still cannot be resolved, the bishop and the standing committee of the diocese adjudicate the matter.

If a congregation has recurring problems, the bishop has authority to prescribe certain experiences designed to bring corrective changes within the vestry or congregation. He can, for example, say that he plans for the congregation to have an interim rector for two years. During that period, the congregation will have consultation and work through whatever is causing the problem. The bishop has the authority to enforce this action, for he can refuse to approve another rector until they deal with the issue(s).

The Presbyterian Church (U.S.A.)

The Presbyterian Church (U.S.A.) probably has developed the most comprehensive set of materials for pastor nominating committees of any denomination at this time. Some definitions and descriptions of Presbyterian polity will be helpful in understanding the following discussion.

All the elected elders of a local congregation make up the session, which is their ruling board, similar to a deacon board in Baptist churches. (A congregation may have forty ordained elders in its membership; however, the session is composed only of the elders elected by that local congregation.)

The presbytery is the judicatory (or governing body) of the Presbyterian Church. The presbytery is composed of all the ministers in a geographic region, whether or not they are presently pastoring churches. Each church in that region is represented by at least one elder on the presbytery. Large churches may be represented by more than one elder. The Presbyterian Church is connectional: individual congregations are under the authority of the regional presbytery.*

When a pastor resigns, the session calls a congregational meeting, and the congregation elects a pastor nominating committee. The session charges the committee with the responsibility for finding one or more candidates to recommend to the church. A denominational staff person will meet with the committee to go over the process of finding a new pastor. This person also serves as a liaison between the pastor nominating committee and the presbytery. The employment process is a three-way process involving the pastor, church, and presbytery. There must be acceptance and approval by all three for a call to occur.

The congregation's committee does a self-study and uses the results of this self-study to complete a Church Information Form. The session and the presbytery review the self-study for accuracy. The committee then sends the Church Information Form to the denominational offices in Louisville. Denominational staff enter it into a computer bank there.

Many pastors within the denomination have completed a Personal Information Form, and these forms are also in this computer bank. Denominational staff forward the Personal In-

*The word *presbytery* is used in at least two senses. The first sense, the governing body, has been described above. The second sense is that the presbytery includes all the churches and ministers and congregational members of a given area.

formation Forms of those pastors whose background and experience match the needs of the church to the nominating committee. The committee also uses other ways of identifying possible candidates, including leads from the presbytery and from the congregation. Some pastors hear of the vacancy and ask to be considered for the position.

After reviewing the Personal Information Forms, the committee members may call or write to references of those pastors they are considering and may call the pastor himself for further information. From these activities, the committee makes the first decisions.

The committee often contacts one or more of the remaining applicants to ascertain their willingness to consider a move. If they express interest, the committee asks for further information, such as tapes of worship services, sermons, bulletins, and newsletters. After reviewing these, committee members usually decide to visit one or more pastors in their home churches and observe them conducting a worship service. They may ask for an interview during the afternoon of the Sunday on which they are visiting. If an afternoon interview is not possible, the pastor and the committee arrange another mutually convenient time. This meeting may sometimes be at the committee's home church so that the pastoral candidate may have an opportunity to see the church buildings and community.

Once the nominating committee has decided it would like to place a candidate's name before the congregation and a candidate affirms his willingness to accept a call if offered, the committee and the candidate negotiate a salary and benefit package. If these negotiations can be concluded satisfactorily, the nominating committee asks the liaison with the presbytery to request permission for a call to be issued. The presbytery has access to a pastor's ordination papers and to other means of evaluating a candidate's theological positions and ministry performance. Therefore, the presbytery can provide a second means of assessing the candidate's orthodoxy and fitness for a particular congregation. After the presbytery approves a candidate, the nominating committee informs the session that it is ready to make a recommendation to the congregation. A date is set for this meeting. At that meeting the committee makes a report to the congregation, and the congregation votes either for or against the recommended candidate. The congregation must give a majority vote for a call to be extended to a pastor.

If a conflict arises within a pastor-congregation relationship, the first step is for the session (the elders and the pastor) to try to resolve the problem. If the problem continues, the presbytery can become involved in trying to solve the issue. The presbytery attempts to provide objective conflict resolution. If it believes the pastor is no longer preaching orthodox theology, it has the power to withdraw his ordination. If it believes that a pastor must move to preserve the congregation, it will usually recommend that the pastor move. The presbytery serves three main functions in these processes—it safeguards doctrinal purity and protects the rights of the church and the pastor.

In the Orthodox Presbyterian Church (but not the Presbyterian Church, U.S.A.), if the presbytery believes that an individual other than the pastor is causing the conflict, it may bring charges against that individual to the local session. Then the local session must determine whether to investigate the charges and administer church discipline. The Orthodox Presbyterian Church is one of the few denominations that continues to use formal church discipline when the actions of an individual seem to warrant it. Charges do not have to initiate from the presbytery. Any local session may initiate the process if they believe it is necessary.

Congregational Selection, Congregational Autonomy (No Congregational Oversight by the Judicatory)

Many denominations are within this category. These include most Baptist churches, Assemblies of God, Churches of Christ,[1] the Christian Church, and most independent congregations. Because there is no denominational oversight, each congregation is free to act as it chooses. For that reason, there is broad diversity, and no generalizations will be true for all.

Southern Baptist

When a pastor resigns or is removed, the congregation usually chooses a pulpit committee to conduct the pastoral search. Frequently the deacon board serves as the pulpit committee. Sometimes the pulpit committee includes members of the deacon board and others who represent various ministries or groups in the church.

The extensiveness of the search often depends on the size, location, and educational level of the congregation. Small, rural congregations may confine their searches to their locality or to their state and often find a new pastor in three to six months. Larger churches often conduct searches that take longer (six to eighteen months) and may look at candidates from several states.

After the committee has identified one or more strong candidates, members usually go to hear each one preach in his home church. The committee may try to interview him that afternoon if there is considerable distance between the two churches and if that can be arranged. When the pulpit committee feels positive about a candidate and he has expressed a willingness to be considered for the church, the pulpit committee usually confers with the finance committee and develops a salary and benefit package to offer him.

The candidate sometimes comes to the church Friday night and spends the weekend meeting various members and groups within the congregation. He may spend only Sunday with the congregation. He preaches Sunday morning and sometimes Sunday evening. The congregation usually votes to call or not to call after the morning or evening service. If the candidate accepts the call, he resigns from his present congregation and makes plans to move to his new church. Many Southern Baptist churches have a period of only two weeks between the resignation and the date it is effective, the shortest of any denomination found in this study (the most common is four weeks, with some denominations recommending six to eight weeks).

If conflicts arise between a pastor and the congregation (or the deacon board), there is an attempt to work them out at that level. The nature of the attempt depends on the personality of the pastor, the focus of the conflict, how widespread the dissatisfaction is, and the personalities of those who disagree with the pastor. In such instances the connectional system provides more safety for the pastor than does the autonomous congregational system. In the connectional system, denominational personnel can come in and attempt to provide some objective mediation of the dispute. Within the autonomous congregational system, two or three persons who determine to pressure the pastor to leave can often effect his termination or make the situation so uncomfortable that he will eventually resign.

Associational personnel (the regional judicatory for Southern Baptists) are willing to be involved in helping a congregation resolve a conflict, but they can come into a local church only by invitation, and they have no authority to implement their suggestions or advice within the congregation. Most pastors realize that if a small group has decided to demand their resignation, mediation is likely to have little effect, so they resign. This is likely to occur even if the vast majority of the congregation are satisfied with the pastor's work. Probably the failure of most congregationally autonomous denominations (not just Southern Baptists) to have adequate safeguards for pastors against a disenchanted few is a weakness of this kind of polity.

Churches of Christ

The Churches of Christ are extremely congregational in nature and therefore diverse in their procedures. They are unique in several ways, ways that are standard in many other congregational and connectional denominations. Their polity generally operates in the following way.

In Churches of Christ the pastor's emphasis is on the pulpit ministry. The *elders* of the church are primarily responsible for counseling, visiting the sick, and developing the spiritual direction of the church. The elder body meets weekly, and individual elders usually spend several hours per week fulfilling their responsibilities. Deacons are responsible for taking care of the practical ministries of the church.

If a pulpit becomes vacant, the elders usually select a search committee. The denomination lacks a centralized board; therefore, no national list of pastoral candidates is available. People learn of the pastoral vacancy through networks and through denominational periodicals. The screening process varies from church to church. Probably very few would conduct a self-study and develop a highly specific pastor profile, as is customary in some denominations.

When the search committee has identified one or more strong candidates, the elders, in consultation with the other associate staff, make the decision about who is to become the new pulpit minister. There is no hierarchical relationship between the pulpit minister and the associate staff. Each is accountable directly to the elders. If the pulpit minister is the newest member of the pastoral staff, he accommodates to them rather than they to him. The power resting with the elders instead of the pulpit minister produces a very different kind of polity from that of most congregational churches. Consequently, associate staff are not expected to resign when a new pulpit minister is called, as is common in many congregational denominations.

If conflict develops between a pastor and the congregation, a wide range of approaches may be used because of the diversity of the churches within the denomination. The elders would obviously play a key role in addressing conflicts at an early stage and in resolving conflicts. Firings or forced resignations reportedly occur rarely in the denomination.

Some Thoughts on the Theological Basis for Decision Making When Selecting a Pastor

How do we find God's will for our lives? How do we find God's will when selecting a pastor? Does God have a perfect will in this matter—one person who will make the best pastor for our church at a given time?

The Traditional View of God's Will

If we read ten books on finding God's will, nine of them probably will teach that God has a perfect will for each step of our lives. We have the responsibility to find that perfect will and follow it. We may do so using road signs such as God's Word, the inner prompting of the Holy Spirit, circumstances, and counsel from mature believers. Because this viewpoint is so common, it has been called the traditional view.

In 1980 Garry Friesen wrote a book called *Decision Making and the Will of God: A Biblical Alternative to the Traditional View*. This book has spurred much discussion among Christians, and much of that discussion is relevant to the topic of pastoral selection. In the following paragraphs I will present a summary of Friesen's discussion.

In normal conversation we use the term *God's will* in three different, yet generally accepted ways. *God's sovereign will* refers to God's predetermined plan for everything that happens in the universe. Everything that happens is a result of divine causation or divine permission and therefore occurs within God's sovereign will. (God's sovereign will could be illustrated by a large circle; everything that happens occurs within this circle.)

A second way we use the term is to refer to *God's moral will*, that is, God's moral commands as revealed in the Bible, which teaches us how we ought to believe and live. This could be pictured as a smaller circle within the larger one mentioned above. Everything that happens according to God's moral plan occurs within this second circle. The area within the larger circle that is not within the smaller circle refers to incidents that God sovereignly allows but are not according to His moral will (for example, all sinful acts).

The term also refers to *God's individual will*—the ideal, detailed life plan that God has uniquely designed for every believer. The life plan includes every decision we make in life (like a blueprint). It is called *God's perfect will* because it is in harmony with the Bible and is the perfect life plan to bring happiness and spiritual success to an individual. It is known as *God's specific will* because it reveals how each specific decision should be made. It is called *God's ideal will* because it shows the ideal life plan for every situation. It is also known as *the very center of God's will*. It could be visualized as a dot in the very center of the two circles mentioned above. According to this view, if a person marries a believer who is not the one God selected, the person would be within the second circle but not precisely on target. This is sometimes called *God's second best* or *God's permissive will*.

Does Scripture Teach a Specific Life Plan for Every Believer?

Few, if any, evangelical theologians doubt the existence of the two outer circles (God's sovereign will and His moral will). However, many evangelical theologians and laypersons, including Friesen, are beginning to question the idea that God has an ideal, detailed life plan for each believer.

In his book Friesen carefully examines every scriptural reference that people have interpreted to mean that God has an individual will for every believer. In each case he shows that when interpreted in its context, the verse that seemed to teach that God has a blueprint for each believer is actually talking about God's general moral will for all believers.

Why then, if the Bible does not teach that God has a detailed life plan for every believer, has this theory been accepted by so many Christians for such a long time? Friesen responds with one possible reason: an imprecise synthesis of biblical teaching and biblical examples.

1. Biblical examples: Scripture tells us that God occasionally guided believers in very specific ways, for example, Paul's Macedonian vision or Jonah's missionary call.

2. Biblical teaching: Scripture also contains God's promises of guidance to believers. (These were promises that God would guide believers into His general moral will but were often interpreted as promises to guide them into His individual will.)

3. Synthesis: God has a detailed life plan for every believer into which He will lead each one who is willing.

There are two major logical fallacies with this synthesis. First, God's occasional leading of believers to a very specific action does not mean that He has a specific blueprint for every step in our lives. Second, God's promise of guidance in the moral decisions of our lives does not mean that He promises to give similar guidance in every nonmoral decision we have to make.

Friesen goes on to point out that the verses usually used to support the traditional (blueprint) view do not support it, and there is no place in Scripture where God clearly teaches the traditional view. If the traditional view is correct, it is so significant that we should surely expect it to be taught thoroughly and fully in one or more places in Scripture. Yet it is not. Our conclusion must be that Scripture teaches the outer two circles—God's sovereign will and His moral will—but not the dot (God's individual life plan). The Bible does teach us that God will guide us, but His promised guidance is in terms of general moral principles, not in terms of specifying every life decision.

The Wisdom View: An Alternative to the Traditional View

If God does not have a specific blueprint for our lives, on what basis are we to make decisions? Friesen's answer can be described in terms of three principles:

1. In those areas the Bible specifically addresses, the revealed commands of God (His moral will) are to be obeyed.

2. In those areas where the Bible gives no command or principle (in nonmoral decisions), the believer is free and responsible to choose his course of action. Any decision made within the moral will of God is acceptable to God.

3. In nonmoral areas, the objective of Christians is to make decisions based on what is most spiritually wise. We are to make decisions based on factors such as how the decision will affect our ability to develop Christian character and honor God with our lives.

Is There Biblical Support for the Wisdom View?

Scripture describes several instances where the apostles made decisions based on what appeared to be the wiser spiritual course to take. For example, on his second missionary journey, Paul founded a church at Thessalonica but was expelled from that town by jealous Jews (see Acts 17:10–15). Paul, Silas, and Timothy knew that the church there would be persecuted and would not have the benefit of experienced leadership. Therefore, they agreed on a plan by which the church could be encouraged and strengthened:

> So when we could stand it no longer, we thought it best to be left by ourselves in Athens. We sent Timothy, who is our brother and God's fellow worker in spreading the gospel of Christ, to strengthen and encourage you in your faith, so that no one would be unsettled by these trials (1 Thess. 3:1–3 NIV).

What was the basis of their decision? "We thought it best"—their basis was sanctified wisdom.

Similarly, when Paul was imprisoned at Rome, the Philippian church sent a love gift to him via Epaphroditus. While in Rome, Epaphroditus became very sick and almost died. After he recovered, he became worried when he heard how concerned his home church was for him, and he also became homesick. Paul decided to send him home with the following instructions: "Yet I considered it necessary to send to you Epaphroditus, my brother, fellow worker, and fellow soldier, but your messenger and the one who ministered to my need; since he was longing for you all, and was distressed because you had heard that he was sick" (Phil. 2:25–26). What was the basis for Paul's decision? "I considered it necessary" or "I thought it wise" in terms of the needs of the moment.

Late in Paul's ministry the Jewish believers in Judea went through a critical famine. Paul encouraged the gentile churches to take up a collection for their Jewish brothers. After the collection was taken, he said he would decide whether to accompany the gift himself:

> On the first day of every week, each one of you should set aside a sum of money in keeping with his income, saving it up, so that when I come no collections will have to be made. Then when I arrive, I will give letters of introduction to the men you approve and send them with your gift to Jerusalem. If it seems advisable for me to go also, they will accompany me (1 Cor. 16:2–4 NIV).

On what basis would he make his decision? "If it seems advisable."

A problem that arose within the early church was the complaint that some believers were not being treated fairly in the daily distribution of food. Luke recounts the situation:

> In those days when the number of disciples was increasing, the Grecian Jews among them complained against the Hebraic Jews because their widows were being overlooked in the daily

distribution of food. So the Twelve gathered all the disciples together and said, "It would not be right for us to neglect the ministry of the word of God in order to wait on tables. Brothers, choose seven men from among you who are known to be full of the Spirit and wisdom. We will turn this responsibility over to them and will give our attention to prayer and the ministry of the word" (Acts 6:1-4 NIV).

What was the basis for the apostles' decision? They believed it *would not be right* for them to lay aside their God-given priorities and become involved in administrative tasks.

In each case, and in others that we do not have time to discuss in a summary of this sort, the apostles did not say they made a decision to do one thing or another because it was God's individual will for them. They explained the rationale for making their decisions based on spiritual priorities: Which alternative would accomplish the spiritual needs of the moment most effectively? The evidence for the "wisdom view" is not confined to descriptive passages alone; believers are encouraged to be spiritually wise in the prescriptive passages in Scripture as well (e.g., Deut. 1:13; Eph. 5:15-16; Col. 4:5). In both lists of criteria that churches were to use in choosing pastors, they were to be sensible and prudent (1 Tim. 3:2; Titus 1:8).

The Wisdom View and Pastoral Selection

How does all this relate to choosing a pastor? If the traditional (blueprint) view is correct, there would be one person in all the world who would be God's perfect choice for a church at any given time. The pastoral selection process would become the almost impossible task of finding that one person.

If the wisdom view of making decisions is correct, it would mean that the choice of any pastor who fits the criteria found in 1 Timothy and Titus is within the moral will of God and therefore is acceptable to God. However, the choice of some pastors for a given congregation may be spiritually wiser than others. For example, it is wiser to choose a pastor whose gifts complement the pastoral needs of a church than it is to choose a pastor who does not have some gifts needed by that church. It would be wiser to find a pastor whose expectations of the pastoral role closely approximate the expectations of the church members than it would be to choose a pastor whose expectations widely diverge from those of the congregation.

Friesen's wisdom view of decision making is compatible with the procedures recommended in the following chapters. By doing a self-study, by developing a pastor profile, by researching a pastor's gifts and expectations and comparing them with the needs and expectations of our congregation, we make a spiritually wiser choice than if we neglect any of these steps.

Learning from Others

Probably the most efficient way of preventing ourselves from making mistakes in a given task is to study the mistakes of those who have gone before us. Santayana is well known for saying that "he who doesn't learn from history is bound to repeat it." For that reason the following chapter identifies mistakes that have frequently been made in the pastoral selection process.

2

Common Mistakes of Pulpit Committees

The purpose of this chapter is not to be critical. Most people who serve on a pastor nominating committee are doing so for the first time in their lives. This also may be the first time they have ever taken part in any kind of employment selection process. Most serve sacrificially and give the very best of themselves to the process. Since the process is complex and since most of us who serve are novices, we will make mistakes. The purpose of this chapter is to help us learn from others' mistakes so that we will make fewer of them.

There continue to be valid differences of opinion about many areas of the pastoral selection process. I have tried to leave those areas for discussion as they come up in the following chapters (not in this chapter). The areas listed in this chapter are probably ones where there is greater consensus that these are mistakes and that there are better ways of handling such situations. If I, while identifying what I believe are mistakes, happen to mention your favorite approach, please forgive me. I hope that you can see beyond our disagreement on that particular issue and benefit from the other ideas mentioned in the chapter.

The mistakes discussed in this chapter refer to those that can be made by pastor nominating committees in the last three categories of church polity discussed in chapter 1. They are not relevant for those denominations where the judicatory screens and appoints pastors, as in the United Methodist Church or the Church of God.

This chapter will be divided into three main parts—mistakes in developing the composition of a pastor nominating committee, mistakes that arise from a failure to do an adequate self-study or develop a careful pastor profile, and procedural mistakes in the working of the committee. For the sake of brevity, the pastor nominating committee, or whatever alternate name it is given in your congregation, will be abbreviated PNC from now on.

Mistakes in Developing the Composition of a PNC

Failure to Represent Important Subgroups

Two groups of people are often not represented on a PNC—older Christians and women. I believe, with others I interviewed, that it is a mistake to leave either group unrepresented. Having seen many pastors come and go, older Christians often have a wealth of wisdom. They may have served on PNCs before and can bring their knowledge of those experiences to this committee. They also represent a growing portion of the population the church should serve. For these reasons I believe it is wise to have older Christians represented on the committee.

Women are the majority in most churches today, and therefore deserve representation. In addition, many women have an intuitive sense of character and are able, after a two-hour discussion with an applicant, to sense that there is something not right about an applicant's character or presentation, though they may not have the historical information to document their intuition. Women often sense this kind of thing accurately when we men miss these signals. As with older Christians, it's unwise to deprive ourselves of their insights.

In some conservative denominations there may be a belief that women should not serve on a PNC because that would constitute a woman having authority over a man and would contradict the apostle Paul's teaching in 1 Timothy 2:12. I do not think this verse prohibits women from serving on such committees, for *no individual member* of the committee, male or female, has authority over the pastoral applicant. Even *the entire committee,* in most denominations, does not have authority over the applicant. It serves as *a nominating committee* and does not make the decision to call or not to call. Therefore, I do not think there is a need, even with the most conservative theology, to exclude the valuable ministry of women from PNCs.

Failure to Carefully Select Members

Another mistake regarding the composition of PNCs is the failure to carefully select the members. Often the congregation determines the makeup of the committee by popular election. Sometimes a standing committee (e.g., the deacon board) becomes the PNC. The PNC's activity will probably be the single most influential work any committee in the church will do in affecting the quality of the church's life for the next five to ten years. For this reason I think more care needs to be taken in its composition.

People chosen for this committee should have a genuine concern for the *whole* church. They should be people who are strong enough that they will not yield to special interest groups. Their judgment should be respected by the congregation. They should be people who can work well as group *members*. Avoid people who dominate discussions or who are verbal and opinionated. Group members should not be people with an ax to grind or people with a history of being divisive. They should be known for their objectivity and fairness.

If you are considering placing individuals on a PNC who have served on such a committee before, keep in mind that they should not be persons who will view themselves as "experts" because of prior service. They should realize that there may have been significant changes in the congregation, the community, and the gifts a pastor needs to minister effectively since the time of their earlier service.

People nominated to a PNC should be aware of the considerable commitment such an appointment requires. It is not uncommon for committees to meet thirty times during their life span. Their responsibilities usually include a few hours of work each week preparing for these meetings. In most denominations the committee will work from six to twelve months before completing its task, and in some denominations (e.g., the Presbyterian Church [U.S.A.]), its task often lasts between one and two years. Nominees to this committee should be people who can devote the considerable time needed, are *willing* to devote this much time, and have the quality of endurance.

Committee members also should be able to keep confidences. At times they will have access to information that, if divulged, could seriously damage careers and ministries. (This does not mean that they will be privy to all sorts of unethical behavior by pastors; a pastor's willingness to be considered for another church could be destructive if it becomes known to the wrong people.)

During the self-study, committee members will need to reexamine how they've always thought about their church's ministry or how they've always done things. This study is important if the church is not to repeat what has been done in the past. If a person's favorite phrase is, "But that's how we've always done things," he or she is probably not a good candidate for the committee. In addition, committee members should be able to represent the church in a professional way.

Several authorities recommend that the committee be composed of an odd number of people to prevent tie votes. I don't necessarily agree with this advice. In reality most PNCs operate by consensus anyway, and usually after discussion there is a clear consensus in one direction or another. If the committee divides evenly on an issue, it probably needs more discussion of the issue rather than simply someone to break the tie vote.

Looking at the above list of criteria, you can see that it is unlikely that a congregation can choose such a group through nomination from the floor and popular election. I think it is wiser to have the board of the church appoint such people. If your church constitution decrees that they be elected, the board can prepare a list of recommended nominees with these qualifications, give the congregation a short education on the significance of this committee and the qualities people should have to serve effectively on it, and then have the congregation elect the committee from the list of nominees.

Mistakes that Arise from a Failure to Do an Adequate Self-Study or Develop a Careful Pastor Profile

There are several reasons why most *congregational* churches (category four from the last chapter) don't do a self-study in preparation for calling a pastor. First, some churches have never heard of one; second, if they've heard of such a thing, they don't see the value of conducting one; and third, they're in a mild panic that if they don't get a new pastor quickly, people will quit coming, tithes and offerings will decrease dramatically, and probably the church will go into receivership.

Episcopalians and Presbyterians (category three from the last chapter) generally do a self-study and develop a pastor profile. They follow this procedure not because they're more spiritual or smarter than category four church members but because their judicatories won't allow them to proceed further with the pastoral selection process until they do.

What are the advantages of adding these two components at the beginning of a search? What are the mistakes we could make if we omit them?

The Fit of the Pastor, the Congregation, and the Community

If we don't do a self-study, we can make the mistake of not considering how the congregation, the new pastor, and the community will fit together. Imagine, for a moment, a visual representation of this process. Let's say that the church is composed of 90 percent squares and 10 percent circles (squares and circles can represent any two significant features that people differ on). The community is composed of 90 percent circles and 10 percent squares. What will happen if you select a pastor who is a hexagon? Will he be effective in witnessing and bringing some of those circles into the church? If he is effective and your church becomes 40 percent circles and 60 percent squares, how will the squares react? Will they expect your hexagonal pastor to become more of a square and put some pressure on those circles to become more squarish as well?

What if you select a square pastor? Will he allow you to remain lethargic about a witness to your community since they're so different from you and him that they'd probably be unreachable anyway? What about selecting a rectangular pastor? He's somewhat attractive because he's different in some ways but not so different from the squares in the church to be a threat. Will he challenge you to become something greater than you are? Will he have a chance to relate meaningfully to the circles outside the church, or will he be so different that he can't communicate effectively to them?

Obviously, geometric figures can't illustrate the complexities of people, but this little example can help us begin to think about how we as a church are in relation to most of those in our community and about the dynamics that occur when we bring in a third person, the pastor, we hope can communicate effectively to both groups. Unless we do an adequate self-study, we won't think carefully about these issues.

What Kind of Pastor Will Challenge Us to Grow Personally?

Related to this is another mistake that we are likely to make if we don't prepare a careful self-study: we don't identify the kind of person who will challenge us to grow. Suppose, for example, you're a member of a conservative denomination that has historically been non-Pentecostal. Recently, however, there has been an influx of several families who are charismatic, although quietly so. Some young people have shown an interest in them, and rumors are that a few of them have received the "baptism in the Spirit." You and most of the congregation have known all the arguments against the charismatic movement since you were twelve. Yet they seem to have a joy, a sense of a personal, vibrant relationship with the Lord that you haven't felt for a long time and that you know many of your fellow church members haven't felt for a long time, either.

If you represent the majority in your congregation by squares and the charismatic minority by circles, what kind of pastor do you want to select? You can select a square, preferably a strong square, who will make sure the charismatic group realize that the church does not recognize the validity of their "experience." You and the other squares surely have the votes to manage this. Perhaps if he's a strong-enough square, those circles will recognize this church isn't the one for them and will go somewhere else. Things will be more comfortable if everyone at First Church is a square.

In your self-study you could come to another conclusion. Suppose you decided that these circles were sincere, genuine Christians much like you. You could look for a pastor who would be willing to help the charismatic and the noncharismatic groups within your church examine this together in an attitude of mutual respect and caring. You could decide that finding a pastor who could help you learn to accept and love Christians who are different from you is a vital next step in your congregation's growth. You and the selection committee realized that this task is not just about charismatic-noncharismatic issues, but it's about how you relate to all Christians who are different from you. If so, your self-study would have helped you make an important different kind of choice than if you had simply looked for another "square" to replace your last square pastor.

Should Our Present Programs Be Redirected?

Another mistake that can happen if we don't do a careful self-study is that we may not reexamine our church and its present programs to see if they need to be refocused. The church mentioned earlier is a good example. Built in the center of town when most of the middle class lived a short distance from downtown, it continued to offer programs geared to upper-middle-class intact families. It had experienced continuing attendance decreases as the families who were the focus of its ministries moved further and further away. Part of the self-study for this church must answer the questions, Do we want to move our church to the suburbs and continue to offer the same ministries that we have in the past, or do we want to remain downtown and start offering some additional ministries that will be attractive to those who currently live close to the church? How will we feel if those new ministries are effective and our church starts to include more of the people who live downtown? Are we willing to make those adjustments, or will we transfer our membership to a suburban congregation that includes people "more like us"? Only by answering these admittedly difficult questions can we start to define the kind of pastor that we need to lead our church in the next step of its growth.

Self-Study Should Include the Whole Congregation

When a church is reexamining its mission and the challenges it is facing now, including input from the entire congregation has several advantages. First, the entire congregation become involved in the self-study. Second, they see the care that the PNC is using as it begins its work. Third, they feel involved in the process; people are more likely to support the *results* of a process if they have had input into the process itself. Fourth, those who are nominated to the PNC may be unaware of some of the strategic challenges facing the church.

For example, Church B was located in an upper-middle-class neighborhood but drew people from a wide geographic area. Many people who lived outside the neighborhood of the church came from middle-class backgrounds. Those from the neighborhood of the church tended to socialize more with one another than they did with people from farther away. Because it was easier for them to be involved, they also provided more of the leadership of the church. The pastor tended to spend more of his time with this group for the same reasons. Without intending to be cliquish, this group and the pastor appeared to be a clique to a significant group of those attending the church from outside the neighborhood, and as a result some of the people left the church over a period of years. The leadership of the church appeared to be unaware that this perception existed; it would likely be identified during a self-study only if the self-study encouraged input from the entire congregation.

Failure of Church Members to Personalize Their Mission

We generally are more likely to act on those issues about which we have personally struggled than those about which we have passively accepted information from others. Therefore, we as church members are less likely to be actively involved in the mission of a church if we have just passively continued doing the activities of those who preceded us. Active involvement in a self-study causes us personally to think through what missions we believe our church should be committed to, and as a result we are more likely to become actively involved. Our motivation comes from inside because we have personalized the mission.

Making a Choice of the Next Pastor Based on a Reaction to the Last One

If we fail to do an adequate self-study and develop a careful pastor profile, we may look for a clone of our last pastor, or we may look for the opposite of our last pastor. If we liked our last pastor, we're likely to look for a clone of him, five to ten years younger, without questioning whether someone like him can best lead us in the tasks facing our church now and in the coming years. If we disliked our former pastor, we usually want someone who is the opposite of him, though the church may not need someone with those characteristics and might even be hurt by someone like that.

Thinking We Have Consensus When We Don't

Another problem that results when PNCs don't become specific about their expectations is that each member has preconceptions about what the church needs and thinks that everyone else shares them. Then when members evaluate candidates, it soon becomes apparent that they do not agree on the criteria needed for someone to be an acceptable candidate. At this point, if the committee is to make further progress, members must go back and develop some criteria for a pastor profile that they can agree on. It may mean that committee members need to compromise on some of their personal preferences. Some PNCs have been known to spend two or three years trying to find a suitable candidate because individuals or subgroups with mutually-incompatible preferences kept vetoing one another's candidates.

Failure to Have Clear and Realistic Expectations

A common reason for the souring of pastor-congregation relationships is the failure to meet each other's expectations. Two of the most common reasons that a pastor fails to meet the congregation's expectations are that (1) the congregation never communicated expectations clearly or (2) the congregation's expectations were unrealistic. Identifying our expectations through a pastor profile reveals unrealistic expectations and allows a candidate to know what we expect of him and whether those expectations are compatible with how he feels he can best minister to a congregation. For example, a PNC might list as some of their expectations:

1. Presence and availability at the church during regular working hours.

2. Well-prepared, challenging sermons Sunday morning, Sunday evening, and Wednesday evening.

3. Regular visitation of the hospitalized and ministry to their families during surgery or medical crises.

4. Effective church administration and management.

5. Counseling and ministry related to marriages, baptisms, and deaths.

Even if the list stopped here, which it never does, the PNC should recognize the unrealistic expectations embedded within it. Most experienced pastors say that preparing three well-developed sermons per week requires at least twenty hours of uninterrupted time. Is the church board willing to designate that the morning hours are the pastor's study time, and he is not to be interrupted during those times except for emergencies?

The ministries of hospital visitation, funeral preparation, and counsel to a family after a death will take him out of the church office for several hours each afternoon. He may find that trying to work and prepare for board meetings or other activities in his church office is highly inefficient because many people want to stop and chat when they see he's in. Thus, the PNC may need to recognize that for their future pastor to accomplish expectations 2 through 5 of the above list, they may need to relinquish totally expectation number 1.

Although the above example is hypothetical, it illustrates

that making expectations specific allows a future pastor (especially if he is an experienced pastor) to point out expectations that he may be unable to fulfill (or that no human could fulfill) and that therefore need to be adjusted.

Procedural Mistakes in the Working of a PNC

Confidentiality

One mistake that PNCs frequently make is the failure from the outset to adopt an explicit code of confidentiality. Such a code should include confidentiality about the identity of applicants the committee is considering, the status of any particular applicant, and the specific reasons for disqualifying a candidate. Adopting such a code has several advantages:

- It protects the ministries of persons the committee is considering.
- It does not allow the congregation to campaign for any specific applicant.
- It does not cause unnecessary anxiety for the present congregations of applicants, some of whom will never even become serious candidates (many committees screen fifty applicants before reaching their final decision; there is no need for all fifty churches to worry about losing the pastor when most of their pastors will not reach the final selection process).
- It protects the self-esteem of applicants the committee does not select (it's hard enough to be rejected by a committee; it's much harder to know that this rejection is public knowledge).

Committee members should probably have a specific statement in mind for use when someone asks them for information. A statement like the following might suffice: "I'd like to answer your question, but because premature public information could damage the ministries of our applicants, we cannot give out specifics. We have received about forty applications for the position and are screening them now (or another general statement that tells the questioner about current activities). When we reach the point that we can present our best candidate to the church, the chairman will give you more details." If the questioner persists, the PNC member can respond, "I'm sorry, but I cannot give out any further details."

Failure to Get a Clear Charge

Unless the PNC is the board of the church, the PNC needs to be given a clear specification of

- what its duties are,
- what authority it has (usually it is only a *nominating committee* and does not have the authority to call a pastor),
- whether it has the authority to negotiate a salary and benefit package (the board or finance committee should probably give the PNC a range to work within for both salary and benefits, with final approval of the package by the board or finance committee), and
- how expenses will be reimbursed (the board should agree to reimburse committee members for all reasonable expenses incurred in communicating with, visiting, and nominating a candidate).

Failure to Adequately Use Denominational Resources

Usually each denominational judicatory, whether connectional or congregational, contains a wealth of information and good advice that can help a committee develop an efficient and wise selection process. Usually denominational officials have an awareness of several possible candidates, and they frequently can, with a few hours of research, identify several more if requested. Because of their relationships with other denominational leaders, they often can obtain important confidential information from them that those leaders might be less comfortable sharing directly with a PNC.

Unfortunately many PNCs, particularly those in congregational denominations, fail to ask for input from their judicatories. One state-level leader of a well-known denomination said; "Most churches in my jurisdiction don't even let my office *know* that they have a pastoral vacancy, much less ask for help in filling it." PNCs may miss out on wisdom and resources that are available simply for the asking.

Not Clearly Organizing the Process at the Beginning

Choosing a new leader for an organization, if done thoroughly, will generate a volume of correspondence, applications, reference contacts, results of telephone and personal interviews, and personal evaluations from each committee member. There will normally be three "cuts" between amassing the initial group of forty to fifty applicants and selecting the top two or three. To add further confusion, pastors will complete their applications at various times over a several-month span.

Unless someone develops a logical, systematic way of identifying where each applicant is in the application and selection process, several problems will develop. Committee members will become confused. Some applicants may get "lost" in the process and not get a fair evaluation. The correspondence between the committee and applicants is likely to become so erratic that applicants get a poor image of the church. In the following chapters a systematic, easy-to-follow process is developed that can be modified to meet the needs of your PNC.

The Interim as an Applicant

If a church has an effective interim pastor, someone will almost inevitably recommend that he become a candidate for the permanent position. As the interim starts to build relationships with the congregation, he also may start to think that he would enjoy being with these people permanently.

The unanimous counsel from denominational leaders is that this candidacy represents a serious mistake. During an interim period people are usually somewhat anxious, for they don't know who their next pastor will be and if they will be able to relate to him. People often choose the security of a known relationship, even when this relationship is not optimal, over the insecurity of an unknown one. They are likely to deny some of the problems they are encountering with the familiar situation because of their need to maintain the security of a known relationship.

Some people will undoubtedly be satisfied if the interim pastor becomes the permanent one, but a very strong likelihood is that allowing this to happen will cause many in the congregation to become dissatisfied with the choice. Church splits or a loss of a significant part of the congregation can occur. A better approach, recommended unanimously by the denominational leaders I interviewed, is for the PNC to ask a potential interim if he wishes to be considered for the permanent position. If he does, he will be considered along with other applicants, but he cannot serve as the interim. The interim, congregation, and committee should know at the outset that the interim pastor cannot become an applicant for the permanent position.

Communication with Applicants

With forty to fifty applicants, chaos can result if more than one committee person interacts with them. Because of the sheer number of names, most of them personally unknown to the committee, remembering who said what to whom becomes impossible.

A better plan is to choose a well-organized chairperson who can spend several hours each week on PNC work and have this person conduct all formal communication between the committee and the applicants. He probably will need to keep a file folder with him on each applicant in which he plots the status of the application and keeps a record of all written and verbal communication. Although this plan obviously requires some time and commitment from the committee chairman, no alternative keeps communication between applicants and committee organized and documented.

Failure to Consider Looking Outside Our Normal Pool of Candidates

A few denominations have national clearinghouses for their ordained clergypersons. For those that do not, it is often helpful to write or telephone the denominational leaders of other states for their recommendations. There are inter-denominational clearinghouses for pastors as well. Mission boards may know of persons who are returning to the States for a variety of reasons. Seminaries and Bible colleges may know of graduates who are involved in ministry but would consider a change. They may also know of graduates who are working in secular settings because they have not found a suitable ministry opportunity. A failure to use these and other sources may result in not finding the best available person for our church.

Failure to Be Honest about Congregational Problems

Probably nothing is so disappointing and frustrating to a newly arrived pastor than to find that his PNC covered up or didn't tell him about significant problems in the church. Our reluctance is understandable. Often we fear that if we are honest, no pastoral applicant will consider us. That is not so. Many leaders see problems as challenges. They enjoy the challenge of helping a disorganized or demoralized group become a satisfied and effective group again. But this is totally different from being led to believe that the group is healthy and functioning well and then finding out that was untrue.

Most pastoral applicants will respond positively to a PNC that is honest about a congregation's problems. Some may see themselves as gifted in dealing with those kinds of problems and will not be discouraged by your honesty. Some will admit that they don't view themselves as gifted in dealing with the kinds of struggles your congregation is facing. They will remove themselves from consideration—a healthy step in the selection process for everyone involved. The wise pastoral applicant will find out about your problems anyway because he'll be checking you out with denominational officials while you're checking him out. He'll undoubtedly be more positively inclined if he hears about a problem from you than if you do not tell him and he hears about it from someone else.

Each committee must decide how to handle this issue. If members decide candidness is the best approach, they must decide at what step in the interview process they will share this information and ask for a response. I would recommend sharing deep problems only with semifinalists and finalists and asking that they keep them in confidence.

Failure to Provide a Church Profile for Applicants

Pastors mentioned this less as a mistake than as a positive step when committees included it. Several pastors who had been considered for numerous pastoral vacancies said that when churches took the time to develop a three- or four-page description of the church for their information packet, it created a positive impression in them and helped them feel that they understood the church better than if they received only statistical information about the church.

Failure to Check References Thoroughly

This mistake was the most important one mentioned by denominational leaders and, surprisingly, by pastors themselves. There is probably a psychological resistance to checking out the references for someone who might become our pastor. As Christians, most of us want to believe the best about others, particularly others in ministry. We may have to overcome some natural antipathy to do a good job here. Most people that applicants list as references do not want to tell bad things about their friend or associate, so they probably won't unless we ask specific and pointed questions. Thorough background checking also involves *checking with people other than those an applicant has listed in his resume.* My interviewees also said that PNCs should check credit history and determine if an applicant has a criminal record. More will be said about how to check out references in the following chapters.

Failure to Prepare Well for Interviews

Several pastors described a scenario similar to this: "I met the pulpit committee at the church at the agreed-upon time. The chairman of the committee had members introduce themselves, then asked if anyone had any questions for me. There was an awkward silence for several minutes, and then someone finally asked a rather elementary question. Committee members followed with a few more questions of about the same depth, each going off in different directions, so that our discussion never went into detail on any topic. I eventually realized that if the interview was going to be of any use to the committee and me, I would have to take over. I did, beginning by describing my education and experience, and then moving into my philosophy of ministry."

The following chapters will include some suggestions on conducting face-to-face interviews with your candidates. You should develop specific goals for each interview, devise questions that will help you accomplish those goals, and decide who will ask what questions and in what order. You don't want the interview to come across as rehearsed, but a well-organized interview will reflect more favorably on your church than one like the interview described in the preceding paragraph.

Failure to Assess Crossover Candidates from Other Denominations with Extra Care

Whenever a person crosses over from one denomination to another a PNC should carefully examine the reasons for the crossover. A person may cross over a denominational line for more than one reason. The stated reason may not be the only one or the most significant one. Thorough checking with denominational officials of the denomination a pastor left may reveal essential information that could bear on whether you will wish to consider this person. It is not uncommon for someone who claims to have left a denomination for theological reasons to have actually left because of immorality or financial mismanagement or unwillingness to be accountable to anyone other than himself. These possibilities need to be carefully checked out.

A person may believe that denominational differences (whether of polity, theology, or parish life) will not bother him when he views our denomination from a distance. However, he may find that they bother him significantly when he is actively involved as a participant/leader. A person who has lived comfortably within the new denomination for several years is more likely to be comfortable as a pastor than one who has recently made the transfer in order to be acceptable as a candidate.

An indication of the importance of this assessment comes from some estimates of pastoral tenure provided by a denominational official in the United Church of Christ. She estimated that in rural pastorates where the pastor was from a United Church of Christ background, the average tenure of pastors was between ten and twelve years. In rural pastorates where the pastor was not from a United Church of Christ background, the average tenure was between one and two years.

Failure to Include Consideration of the Spouse and Children in the Recruitment Process

Secular "executive headhunters" know that a failure to address the needs of the spouse and children can often sabotage an effort to recruit a new executive. Although the motivations of most pastors are not identical to those of secular executives, it is probably equally true that they are not likely to move to a new setting against the strong wishes of the wife and children. An effort should be made to address these needs, beginning with the information packet and continuing throughout the recruitment process. A pastor's wife should be included in the interviews, giving her an opportunity to describe her personal upbringing, her thoughts about ministry, her personal involvement in their church's present programs and, at the end of the interview, an opportunity to ask any questions or voice any reservations. She is much more likely to support her husband's decision to move if she feels she has played an active part in that decision and if she believes the church genuinely cares about her needs and the needs of the children. Also, the members of the PNC get the opportunity to see how well they think she would be accepted as a pastor's wife in their church.

Failure to Be Discreet When Visiting Another Church

Making a personal visit to the candidate's present church to view him in the pulpit is a time-honored tradition in certain denominations, and one that probably will not cease in the near future. However, the way we make a personal visit to another church can be modified. Probably a classic instance of how not to be discreet occurred in a large southern town a few years ago.

The pulpit committee from Church B in another city decided that they wanted Pastor A for their next pastor. Pastor A had a growing ministry in his present church, was deeply loved by his present congregation, and had no interest in being called by another church. Nevertheless, the fifteen members of the deacon board of Church B drove to Pastor A's church one Sunday morning in their oversized church van, with their church's identity conspicuously lettered on its side. They parked in the middle of the parking lot, walked into the church and, staying together, occupied an entire pew in the front center of the church auditorium.

The incident left Pastor A's congregation deeply shaken. They knew they could never compete with what Church B could offer their pastor. They feared that they would soon be losing the pastor they had learned to love and trust.

There is no need for a pulpit committee to behave so insensitively when making a visit to a pastoral candidate's home church. With just a moderate amount of common sense and care, a pulpit committee can visit a church discreetly and courteously. In this way only the ushers and a few board members are likely to become aware of the visit.

Overemphasizing Pulpit Skills

This mistake is the one most commonly mentioned by persons I interviewed. Pulpit skills are certainly important, and according to Peter Wagner, there is no significantly growing church in America that does not have a strong pulpit.[1] However, communication skills are not the only skills necessary for a pastor to have an effective ministry. The pastor must also be emotionally healthy, have good interpersonal skills, be a good trainer and motivator of others, and be a good administrator. Our present methods, which enable most church members to see a candidate only as he preaches one or two sermons, overemphasize one set of skills rather than highlight the total record. They may lead to an unfair evaluation of a candidate who has only moderate pulpit skills but who is, overall, an excellent pastor.

Not Scheduling Enough Time for the Candidate and Congregation to Meet Each Other

Closely related to the previously noted mistake is the way that we schedule the meeting between a candidate and a congregation. Frequently there is no contact except through the sermon and a brief handshake at the conclusion of the Sunday morning service. The congregation are expected to vote on the person who will be their spiritual shepherd for the next several years when they haven't had enough interaction to make an adequate decision. There are many emotional parallels between a marriage and a pastor's relationship with a congregation. Imagine having to make a decision about whether you wanted to marry someone based on hearing the individual make one or two speeches!

The "Beauty Pageant" Approach

Pastors and denominational overseers frequently identified this mistake. A PNC will arrange for several of the top candidates to preach to the congregation on successive Sundays. The congregation vote for their choice after they have heard them all. This approach is likely to lead to church splits or significant dissatisfaction because various parts of the congregation are likely to favor different candidates.

It is true that nominating committees must consider several candidates simultaneously. They may feel unsure of which candidate will be best for their congregation. However, the unanimous consensus is that they should screen the candidates until they have identified the person they believe could best meet the needs of the church and then should present this person to the congregation. Only if the congregation reject this first person should a second candidate be presented.

Panicking When Not Finding a Suitable Applicant

Sometimes the PNC abruptly realizes that six months or nine months or a year has passed since it started working but they have not yet found a strong candidate. This awareness may cause members to forget the standards and criteria they have so carefully developed and recommend someone without proper screening or talents. Church congregations may pick up the PNC's panic, and together they may invite a candidate who doesn't have some gifts the church needs. Unfortunately, a pastor selected in panic usually does not turn out to be a satisfactory pastor for a congregation.

Choosing a Pastor "On the Rebound"

A church was considering a candidate it liked very much who had expressed an interest in coming. The members were extremely disappointed when he made a decision at the last moment to go to another church. Still trying to recover from the disappointment, the church considered another candidate two weeks later without doing a thorough background check and invited him to be the pastor. He accepted.

As it turned out, the new pastor's wife had a serious drinking problem, and he was developing one himself. Shortly after coming to the church he started having an affair. He and his wife divorced, and he married the other woman. Ten years after his arrival, the church is half the size that it was when he started. Neither the PNC nor the congregation adequately screened this pastor, probably because they were still emotionally "on the rebound" from their rejection by a previous candidate.

Not Keeping the Interim Pastor and Associate Staff Informed

For some reason that no one has fully explained, PNCs frequently fail to talk regularly with the interim pastor and the associate staff. As a result, these staff believe that the board doesn't consider them important, and they can become depressed, apathetic, or angry. Probably many churches have lost good associate staff during or after the interim period because of their lack of sensitivity in keeping them informed.

There are emotional reasons for communicating regularly with the staff. In some denominations, churches expect all associate staff to submit their resignations at the time they call a new pastor. The staff need to know how the process is proceeding in order to know how aggressively to pursue their own job searches.

The interim pastor lives with the constant knowledge that his relationship with these church people can be severed at any time. He may have begun to care deeply about some of them. It helps him to know how much to invest himself in these relationships if he has some idea of how long it will be before he has to say good-bye.

Not Allowing Enough Grieving Time

Congregations grieve just as individuals do. If a pastor has been with a congregation only a year or two before he leaves, this grieving may not take long. (In this event there may be more anger at his short tenure than grief unless a good reason for his departure is evident.) However, if a pastor has been with a congregation for ten years or more, the conventional wisdom is that there should be an interim pastor for at least a year. Otherwise the next pastor, who thought he was going to be a permanent pastor, will be an interim pastor, too.

We cannot say with confidence what causes this phenomenon. The idea of the need to grieve is a plausible explanation. The congregation may need to let the memory of their former pastor recede enough in their minds that they are not always comparing the new pastor with him. Or if there was much anger at their former pastor, the anger may need to recede so that it is not unconsciously displaced or transferred onto the innocent new pastor who replaces him.

Not Using the Interim to Address Needed Issues

Most interims will not try to work on issues that may need attention, such as unfinished business from a previous pastorate, grieving, unrealistic expectations, or improper ways of treating a pastor, unless the board asks them to do so. Many interims could help with the healing process if asked. Our failure to ask them to address these issues means that we fail to use them to the full extent that we could. And our church will be less prepared to receive a new pastor than it could be.

Inadequate Communication with Applicants

Applying for a new job creates high excitement/high anxiety for people. For that reason PNCs need to acknowledge having received each application. They should also let the applicant know if any parts of the application still need to be received to complete it. The committee should give the applicant some explanation of the screening process and an estimate of when he may expect to hear from them again. It is sensitive to periodically send a statement of where the committee is in the process and to compassionately contact applicants no longer being considered. Several pastors said that they had friends in the ministry who had made applications for pastoral vacancies but had never received any feedback from the PNCs to which they applied. They also shared how frustrating and demoralizing this experience had been for their friends.

Mishandling Negotiations

Many potential candidates are involved in ministries and satisfied with their present positions. Many factors may make them reluctant to move or even consider moving. PNCs need to recognize that part of their work involves "courting" potential applicants so that they will be willing to make an application. Another part of "courting" involves planning how to respond to questions about the position, its benefits, and so on. PNCs must be knowledgeable about the position and must not antagonize good candidates at any point during the interview or negotiation process. Committees can make progress in this direction by trying to look at their process and what they are offering *from the perspective of the candidate.* If they were the candidate, would they be attracted to the position and salary/benefit package being offered? Also, do they think they would like to work with this church if the persons on the committee are representative of the congregation's members?

Sending Mixed Signals

When we are talking with a finalist and we know he would like to hear that he is number one, it may be hard not to give signals that he interprets to mean he is the top candidate. Unfortunately, the pain he feels when he finds out someone else has been chosen is greater than the momentary excitement when he misinterpreted our statements to him.

In this situation it is probably more loving to very clearly let a candidate know that he is one of the top persons we are considering but we have not made the final decision. It is easier to recover from being a hopeful who lost than from thinking you were number one and then lost.

Failure to Get All Agreements in Writing

There are many opportunities for verbal understandings to become distorted in a person's memory and for verbal agreements not to be passed along to the appropriate person or committee. These situations can easily take the joy out of a positive beginning.

One denomination has a unique way of avoiding such problems. After the PNC and the candidate have reached a satisfactory agreement, each party writes down a complete description of what each believes the agreement to be and sends it to the other. The two parties resolve any discrepancies at this stage. The PNC then sends the written agreement to whatever board has the authority to approve it. The agreement is formally signed if the congregation calls the candidate.

This chapter has dealt with mistakes, and a committee member could easily become overwhelmed by the number of possible mistakes that can be made. However, God in His love often works through our processes, preventing us from making mistakes that we don't have the wisdom to avoid on our own. Also, any single committee rarely makes more than a few of those mentioned above, and some committees make none. I hope that by being prepared, your committee can be one of them.

A summary of the common mistakes pulpit committees make and suggested ways to avoid those mistakes is included as Appendix A.

Guiding the Church
During the Transition Process

During the interim period, ten tasks need to be addressed by either the church board or the PNC, or by the two groups working together.

- One or both groups must work to allay the initial panic and recurring anxiety that a church congregation feels when it is without a permanent pastor.
- The board must appoint or the congregation must elect a PNC and give it a charter and charge.
- With its denominational judicatory or on its own, the PNC must develop a search plan.
- The board, PNC, and congregation must say Good-bye to the pastor and his family not just verbally but also emotionally.
- The board and the PNC must decide whether any psychological issues concerning the pastorate need to be addressed during the interim period. If so, they must decide how they can best address these issues.
- One or both groups must decide whether pulpit supply (having a variety of speakers at the church worship services) or an interim pastor can best meet the church's needs. Someone will need to be designated to work out the details of either choice.

- After the departing pastor leaves, his job description must be examined and all important pastoral duties divided and delegated to someone.
- Worship and teaching experiences must be developed that keep the congregation interested and involved.
- The PNC must develop one or more ways of keeping the board, congregation, interim pastor, and associate staff regularly informed of its progress.
- The board or the PNC must decide the employment status of the associate pastoral staff and discuss that decision with them individually.

These tasks occur in a general sequential order, but the order varies with individual situations, and some tasks run concurrently with other tasks. The following discussion places the various tasks and the decisions that must be made in roughly the order they will be encountered in most interim situations. Some tasks are the responsibility of the board; others, the responsibility of the PNC.

1. The Pastor Announces His Resignation Privately to the Board.

Though not always done, such an announcement is a courtesy when it does occur. The board can recover from its initial disorientation before the pastor announces his resignation to the congregation. And the board can begin its initial work in structuring a PNC.

2. The Board Appoints a Temporary Chair of the PNC and Develops or Revises a Charter and Charge.

Some churches will have a charter and charge already written into their church constitution. For them, the board should review it to see if it needs to be revised and should make such revisions. Some churches will not have any information regarding a PNC in their constitution, so a charter and charge must be developed. Here are some things that need to be included.

Size

Most judicatories recommend an odd number of members to preclude tie votes. As mentioned in the last chapter, most PNCs work by consensus rather than vote anyway. If the committee is so evenly divided that there is a tie vote, the issue probably needs further discussion rather than simply someone to break the tie.

There are differences of opinion about the optimal size of a PNC. These differences probably occur because some denominations rarely do a self-study and pastor profile, and others routinely do them (denominations that regularly do them recommend larger committees). Also, advocates for smaller-sized PNCs usually come from denominations where fewer candidates are available to a PNC. Advocates for larger PNCs usually come from denominations where many candidates are readily available through computerization. It also will make a difference if the self-study is to be done by the PNC or by a separate task force appointed for that purpose.

Thus, a decision about the optimal size of a PNC depends on several factors. For a medium- to large-sized church that plans to do a careful self-study and pastor profile and that has access to many candidates through computerization, I agree with Loren Mead's comment that committees with fewer than six or more than twelve have a hard time doing their work.[1] A small church that does not have many possible candidates to screen may be served adequately by a committee of four to six.

Composition

In some churches the board (session, deacon board, vestry, etc.) makes up the entire PNC, or a majority on it. Several arguments favor this arrangement. First, the congregation already have chosen these people as their leaders. Second, they frequently have more theological background and experience than average congregational members. Third, they frequently have a good understanding of the needs of the congregation.

There are also some disadvantages of having the board become the PNC. First, the board will play a very important role in helping the church maintain a strong worship and teaching program during the interim period. Serving on the board *and* the PNC will cause a significant strain to members. Second, most boards tend, by their nature, to support the thinking and programs of the past. They may not be as open as others to recognize that the present congregation needs some changes. Third, every board has blind spots—unspoken, often unconscious assumptions about the environment, norms, and purposes of the church. Often only as we talk with someone with a different perspective can we become aware of those blind spots. Considering these points, I would recommend that the PNC include both board members and several people representing groups not on the board.

Persons chosen as PNC members should be known for their genuine concern for the whole church and their good judgment. They should be able to work well as group members; that is, they respect others' ideas and are not overly outspoken, opinionated, or divisive. They should be objective and fair and able to represent the church in a professional way.

The church constitution may specify that committee members must be elected or appointed. If they are to be elected, it may be wise for the board to prepare a list of nominees that would represent a healthy and balanced PNC. The board can then submit this slate of candidates to the congregation for a vote.

All nominees to the PNC should be informed about the importance of this committee and told why the board would like to nominate them. The board should inform them about the commitment involved (one weekly meeting and two to four hours of outside work per week) and ask if they would be willing to serve. Whenever appropriate, let them know that they could be relieved of other church responsibilities for the duration of the committee's work.

Procedures to Be Used by the Committee

The charter should specify what the committee is to do, preferably in writing. For example, the committee can screen applicants until they have identified three to five finalists whom they refer to the board for final screening. Or they may work until they can present the board with their most highly recommended candidate, second-highest, and so on. They can be authorized to negotiate salary and benefit packages, staying within guidelines approved by the board, or the board can do this.

The charge should specify whether the PNC will be provided with secretarial support by the church secretaries. It should identify what expenses will be reimbursed in the selection process (for example, mileage and meals when visiting a potential candidate). It should specify what documentation has to be submitted for the expenses to be reimbursed. The charge should also clarify whether the board or the PNC is responsible for deciding to have pulpit supply or an interim pastor. It should tell who is responsible for finding either pulpit supply ministers or an interim pastor. It should indicate how frequently the PNC is to report to the board and the congregation. Any target date set for finding a new pastor should be included.

Appointment of a Temporary Chair

The committee should have the right to choose its own chair, but someone may be appointed temporary chair until the board or congregation has selected the full committee. Quoted below are some excellent suggestions about making this choice:

> The role of the chairperson is to encourage discussion of
> various viewpoints rather than discouraging them; to delegate

responsibility and follow up on tasks, rather than doing all the work alone; to ensure that decisions reached are the consensus of the group rather than the will of the chairperson or of an outspoken minority. The chairperson, therefore, should be someone whom the congregation respects highly, who has proven ability in these areas.[2]

I would add that chairpersons should be able to bring digressive discussions tactfully back on track. They should be excellent organizers who pay attention to details. They should be willing and able to invest several hours per week in committee work.

3. The Pastor Announces the Resignation to the Congregation. The Temporary Chair of the PNC or the Board Chair Addresses the Congregation.

Loren Mead says of this moment:

Confusion and panic are the inevitable results when the pastor announces that she or he has accepted a call or appointment elsewhere. This is true even if the congregation has been through the same thing just a few years ago. It is true if everybody in the congregation was just hoping the pastor would leave. It happens if the pastor has been there two years or thirty.[3]

The chair who addresses the congregation now should not expect anyone to remember what he says nor should he make a long speech. His attitude is more meaningful than his content. He can include helpful comments in his short announcement. He recognizes that people may be experiencing deep feelings about what they have just heard. The board is nominating or appointing a PNC now. The committee will begin work in the next ten days. Pastor X will be continuing in the pulpit for these next four weeks (or whatever is true). After that we will have one or more people who will lead worship and preach until we have found a new pastor. Concluding with a prayer that asks God to guide the church and the PNC during the coming months is likely to reassure the congregation.

4. The Congregation or Board Selects the Remainder of the PNC.

The preceding discussion has already suggested criteria for members of the PNC. If the church constitution allows appointment, this committee can be appointed and can meet during the coming week. If the committee has to be elected, its first meeting will be delayed by at least one week for the following reasons:

- Congregation members will not be emotionally ready to consider and vote on a list of candidates immediately after the pastor's resignation. Therefore, this time would not be appropriate to have the election. Scheduling the election of the PNC immediately after the pastor announces his resignation also seems in poor taste.
- Attendance at the Sunday evening and Wednesday evening meetings of most churches is not large enough to constitute a quorum, so elections could not be held at these times.
- Therefore, the following Sunday morning after the service is likely to be the first time after the pastor's announcement that the quorum necessary for an election can be obtained. Persons elected can meet immediately after the election to decide their first meeting time.

5. Initial Meetings of the PNC Are Held.

At the first meeting, the PNC should usually go over the search process. In some denominations someone from the judicatory provides this information. Even if your denomination's polity does not require it, I would recommend that you invite your regional denominational leader to this meeting. These leaders often have wisdom, experience, and relationship networks that can greatly enhance the effectiveness of your committee. They have seen many churches go through this process, while this is likely to be your first time on a PNC.

There is nothing shameful about feeling ignorant about how to approach the search process. J. William Harbin says, "One of the most important committees in any church is the pastor search committee. Even though many of the finest church members serve on these committees they have probably less information about their work than any committee in the church."[4]

Bunty Ketchum, a highly regarded church consultant, recommends that the committee spend their second session discussing the skills each member brings to the search process and the fears and other feelings of members. Often individuals have only limited awareness of the skills of other committee members; by sharing them, some natural divisions of labor may become apparent. The sharing of feelings and hopes starts to build cohesion between members of the PNC.

Toward the end of the second session is an opportune time to do three more things. First, choose a permanent chairperson. Second, set up a weekly meeting date. The work will proceed more rapidly if the committee meets weekly, scheduling assignments to do between each meeting. To find a mutually possible time, members may have to do some shifting of their schedules, so this discussion may take a bit of time.

Third, encourage all committee members to give up other church activities for the duration of the committee's work. Committee meetings will generally last one and one-half to two hours each week, and committee assignments probably will take another two to four hours per week. Most members will be hard-pressed to be involved in other church activities besides the committee. Right now the most important thing each committee member can do for the church is to find an excellent new pastor as soon as possible. Therefore, it is in the best interest of the church for them to resign from other activities temporarily. Most thorough searches will last from nine to eighteen months—too long for most people to do double duty without burning out.

6. PNC: Decide on an Overall Plan for Your Pastoral Search; Develop Your Own Procedures.

Your initial meeting with the judicatory may have revealed that they have already developed a thorough plan of action, or it may have given you only bits and pieces of good advice without a complete plan. If they have no overall plan, I will recommend one here that will be elaborated in the following chapters; it can be modified to meet your particular situation. Before starting on the initial steps, have a sense of how the entire plan will work. Knowing the entire plan allows you to work efficiently and appear well organized in your contacts with referral sources and applicants. Early steps in the plan, starting with the second session described earlier, would include the following:

1. Choose a chair, vice-chair, and secretary for the committee.

2. Clarify any ambiguous wordings in the charter and charge you have received from the board. Be certain that the board has authorized payment of all reasonable expenses associated with the search committee's work. Have a clear understanding with the board and/or finance committee regarding what salary and benefit ranges you may discuss with applicants. Decide who will negotiate a final financial package and who needs to approve it when complete.

3. Agree on any procedural rules you want to implement.

    a. Agree on confidentiality and suggest ways to respond if someone asks you for specific information about the committee's work.

    b. Decide whether your committee needs to be unanimous before recommending a candidate to the board and the congregation. If not unanimous, what percentage of support must a candidate have from your committee before you recommend him?

    c. Agree that you will not discuss the name of a prospective pastor with the congregation until the commit-

tee is ready to make a recommendation to the church.
d. Agree that no one will be recommended to the church until the committee has heard him preach (either in person or via audiotape or videotape) and the committee has completed a thorough background check.
e. Agree that a prospective candidate will not preach before your congregation until the committee is ready to recommend him to the congregation.[5]
f. Set up a plan for regular communication between PNC, board, congregation, and interim and associate staff.

A time of leadership change is a time of anxiety for everyone in an organization, whether that organization is the church or a secular one. Nearly everyone is asking questions: "Will they find a good leader?" "How will I like that person?" "What effect will the choice of that person have on me?" In a church, where the choice of a pastor affects every person, these questions produce even more anxiety than in a large secular organization where many people will be minimally affected by the leadership choice.

Studies have shown that several factors affect the amount of anxiety a person experiences at this time. The first is available information—people who have access to little or no information are more anxious than those who understand what is happening. A second factor that reduces anxiety is the opportunity to have input—to have a sense of having some control over what is happening.

These two findings have practical implications for our work on the PNC and the way we relate that work to the rest of the church body. Regular, informative reports that tell what the committee is doing can help the congregation see that the committee is proceeding along a well-thought-out, careful plan to find the best possible candidate for the church. Besides reducing anxiety, this information can do much to fend off frustration at the length of time required to make a thorough pastoral search. It also will increase the credibility of the candidate the committee eventually recommends to the congregation. Probably a brief report to the congregation and staff biweekly is sufficient to meet these needs. A written status report in the church newsletter can inform those who miss that service.

Another practical implication of this research is that the congregation's anxiety also will be decreased in proportion to the amount of their input in the decision making. The wise PNC gives the congregation opportunities to have input into its work whenever appropriate. In the pastoral selection model discussed in this chapter, opportunities to ask for congregational input occur at Steps 4, 7, 10, 15A, 15C, 15M, and 15N.

7. Conduct a Self-Study.

The self-study should include, among other things, an identification of the needs of the church now, the needs anticipated in the next five to ten years, situations that are not being addressed adequately now, and visions for ministries for which the church needs to be challenged. Include congregational input.

8. Help the Congregation Say Good-Bye to the Departing Pastor and His Family.

Some churches will have problems associated with the previous pastor that need to be worked through; some will not. However, *every church will have some grieving to do*. Church members will experience several feelings in the first week following the pastor's resignation. Those who did not like the pastor may feel relieved that he is leaving. For those who liked him, the first response may be panic: What will happen to the church now? They may wonder what they did wrong that caused the pastor to leave. They may feel guilty that they didn't give him more support and wonder if he would not have resigned had they given more support and affirmation. Those who are going through crises may be angry that their pastor is leaving just at the time they need him most.

Stages of Grieving

Several years ago Elisabeth Kübler-Ross identified five emotional stages that people often goes through when they find out they have a terminal illness—denial, anger, bargaining, depression, and acceptance.[6] Since the publication of her book, many observers have recognized that people may go through these stages when they are grieving for other things than just their death. Some have applied this model to the process a congregation goes through when they learn that their pastor is leaving.

Denial happens almost immediately for many people. Perhaps they hear via the "grapevine" that their pastor is going to announce his resignation the following Sunday. Their first response may be, "No. That can't be right." Denial is a defense mechanism that often comes into action when we receive information that we're not emotionally prepared to receive. The cancer patient can't believe the first doctor's diagnosis and goes for a second opinion. Similarly, our first response to information that our pastor is leaving may be to doubt the accuracy of that information. This response is less likely when our first inkling of the change comes as the pastor himself announces his resignation. Then it's less possible to use denial to cushion the impact of information we're not emotionally prepared to receive.

People frequently feel *anger* a short time later. As the denial wears off and they recognize that the pastor really is leaving, they may begin to feel angry that he is doing so. Some people feel rejected by the pastor, believing that he's leaving because he prefers another group of people over them. For others, the situation stirs memories of abandonment by people they had trusted. And for people going through a very stressful time in their lives, they feel like they need the support of their pastor right now.

Bargaining is a third stage people often go through when they become aware that a loss is imminent. Cancer patients may attempt to bargain with God, promising Him that if He will cure their cancer, they will stop smoking, live better Christian lives, become missionaries, and so forth. Patients may attempt to bargain with their doctors, volunteering to be available for experimental treatments or anything else that might prolong their lives. Bargaining also may occur when a pastor is leaving. People will sometimes ask a pastor if there is anything they can do to support him more in board or congregational meetings. They may move that he be given a raise. They may demand that the board fix up the parsonage as he and his wife have been requesting for the last three years. Sometimes people will go through this bargaining process mentally and then dismiss this as unlikely to make the pastor change his mind and so never do it verbally.

Depression occurs when people have gone through the denial stage and recognize that the pastor's announced resignation has truly happened. They've gone through the anger stage, where they have vented, either mentally or verbally, their hurt that the pastor is leaving. They've realized that bargaining will not cause him to change his mind. Depression is the result when they fully accept the reality that the pastor is leaving and that nothing will change his decision.

Acceptance is the stage following depression. The persons may not be happy, but they have fully accepted the fact that the pastor is leaving (or has left). They have begun to build a meaningful life without him. The situation is similar to that of a mother grieving over the loss of a child. Now, recognizing that there is nothing further that can be done to bring him or her back, she begins to reinvest her life in the people who are still living.

How long does it take for a person to go through these five stages? That is a highly individual matter. It depends on the person's relationship with the pastor, their general mental healthiness, and whether the person gets "stuck" someplace in the grieving process. One minister knew folks who were still angry with a pastor five years after that pastor's departure.

Does this process have any implications for how long before leaving a pastor should announce his resignation? One denominational leader recommended that it be no more than two weeks. His rationale was that otherwise the congregation starts to make aggressive statements to the pastor that tear him down unnecessarily. I do not believe that two weeks is long enough for healthy good-byes to occur. This denominational leader may have been seeing congregations going through the second stage of the grieving process (anger). Although this situation is uncomfortable for the pastor, most pastors should be emotionally healthy enough to recognize that this is a normal part of the grief process, and that at least some people who make angry statements are doing so because they are afraid of what will happen to the church and to them after the pastor is gone. Of course, people will sometimes express anger and criticisms at this time because they have been keeping them pent up. They realize that if they don't say them now, they will never get a chance to say them. These criticisms should be treated like any other feedback; the pastor should thank the person for sharing the perspective and should think about the criticism and possibly use it to make changes in his ministry style.

Loren Mead discusses the problems that can result when a church congregation does not have an adequate opportunity to grieve:

> Avoiding this developmental task will leave the dynamics of grief as new booby traps for the future—anger and bitterness popping up in unexpected places (not unlikely to occur in relationship to the new pastor, whoever she or he may be), a sense of apathy or depression (characterized by loss of energy, pullouts and dropouts unable to commit to any new leadership), bargaining (trying one thing after another to try to make the new parish under the new pastor just like—or just the opposite of—what it was before, whatever "before" one remembers), and avoidance (simply not admitting to any

change at all, and consequently being unable to commit to new life).[7]

If we accept Kübler-Ross's model as a generally accurate model for the grieving process, it is probably healthiest if congregation members can go through the denial, anger, and bargaining stages and be in the depression stage or the beginning of the acceptance stage when the pastor leaves. How long is this likely to take? How long should it be between the time that a pastor announces his resignation and the time he says his last good-bye to the congregation?

Obviously that will depend somewhat on the pastor, the congregation, the nature of their relationship, and the reason for his leaving. I would recommend somewhere between six and twelve weeks.

Three groups may find it especially difficult to go through the grieving process.[8] One group includes those who were especially close to the pastor emotionally. A second includes those who may not have appeared to be close to the pastor but have deep feelings because of something or someone the pastor symbolized in their lives (e.g., the person who never knew his or her father who in some sense "adopted" the pastor as a father figure). A third group, surprisingly, includes those who often opposed the pastor during the pastorate. These people are likely to have conflicted grieving processes because they may (consciously or unconsciously) feel guilty for things they have done. They may feel responsible for the pastor's departure. (This is analogous to the situation of a chronically critical spouse who may experience more than usual difficulty at the death of his or her partner. Guilt feelings often complicate the grieving process.)

The departing pastor should be available for these groups of people to spend individual time with him. He should be especially sensitive to spontaneous remarks or behavior suggesting these people need to have such time. Helping them express these difficult feelings may increase their awareness of other people with whom they've had difficulty saying good-bye. This awareness may spur personal growth in those other relationships as well.

Loren Mead says in this regard:

> Saying "good-bye" is terribly important; too many pastors are self-centered at this point, refusing to let people have parties and occasions for saying good-bye, acting as if the celebrations were for the person of the departing pastor. No way. They are important moments for potential ministry on the part of pastors who are leaving, moments that may make the difference between freeing people for the future or tying them to one's apron strings for years to come.[9]

Besides being sensitive to individuals who may need some personal time to say good-bye and providing that, pastors can do other things that will help either them or the congregation to say good-bye. One recommendation from Lyle Schaller will probably help the outgoing pastor say good-bye to the church and will definitely help the incoming pastor and the congregation during the coming months.[10] Schaller recommends that the outgoing pastor prepare one or more confidential audiotapes. These tapes should include his reflections on the church, its history, its strengths, its problems, and its potential "land mines." This legacy also can include active and inactive membership lists and information about parishioners who need special ministry. The tapes can recount details of successful and unsuccessful programs that he has tried, including a discussion of what the departing pastor believes have been his "six best successes and six biggest defeats." They might include a brief introduction to other pastors in the area.[11]

The tapes could be left with the chair of the PNC, to be given to the new pastor within the first two weeks after his arrival. These tapes are probably the most helpful legacy a departing pastor can leave to help the new pastor provide continuity of care. Obviously a pastor will have more difficulty preparing such tapes if he leaves under negative circumstances rather than of his own volition.

Another structured activity of value here is the PNC's in-depth exit interview with the pastor (and perhaps his spouse). This interview helps the committee in its own grieving process. Also, the pastor and his wife often have significant input to include in the self-study because they have perspectives about the congregation that no one else has.[12]

Exit interviews can be structured in a variety of ways. It is sometimes useful for a neutral third party, such as a denominational consultant, to lead the discussion and help each party "hear" the other, particularly if tensions have developed. The discussion leader should attempt to help the discussion remain nonjudgmental—an honest sharing of perspectives that may help both groups understand and say good-bye to each other.

One obvious topic is the pastor's *true* reasons for leaving. In some situations, the real reasons for a pastor's leaving are disguised in spiritual-sounding language (for example, "We believe God is leading us to another field"), and the PNC and the congregation may fail to recognize some issue in the congregation or the congregation's relationship with the pastor that needs to be addressed. If a congregation has been constantly critical of a pastor and his family and they are leaving for that reason, the PNC needs to know that and address it. If a church is failing to pay its pastor a livable wage and he is leaving for that reason, the most loving thing he can do is to honestly share that.*

The exit interview can be a time for discussing feelings about leaving or being left, expectations that were met or unmet by either party, and the reasonableness of those expectations. If handled well, the exit interview will yield insight, growth, and development for both the pastor and the PNC.[13]

If the departing pastor feels comfortable with this idea, he

*Wm. Bud Phillips in his book *Pastoral Transitions* lists seven possible reasons for a pastor's leaving: professional development, family needs and wants, changes of attitude, shifts in the feelings of "fit" between the pastor and the congregation (or the denomination), increased earning potential, added prestige, and greater challenge (p. v).

can address grieving, "letting go," ministry calls, friendships, and trusting God when we're uncertain of the future. He can do this either directly or indirectly in his sermons or through articles he writes in the church newsletter.

Another structured activity that can help the congregation say good-bye is a farewell reception and liturgy. However, I believe the typical stand-up reception has limited psychological value. Often it primarily becomes just another social gathering of the congregation, with a hastily mumbled "Good-bye, we'll miss you," at the end. An alternative that I think would do much more for the emotional letting-go process of the congregation and the pastor would be to have a sit-down reception. The reception could include humorous skits and serious, short talks where selected members of the congregation reminisce about meaningful and moving events that the pastor and the congregation shared. The laughter, combined with tears, can be a healthy catharsis for everyone.

A liturgy could be developed, if your denomination does not already have one, that could be used to allow the congregation to "send off" the pastor and his family with their best wishes and prayers.[14] Wm. Bud Phillips suggests that the following things be said in a good good-bye:

We will miss you!

There will always be a place for you here, even though it will not be the same place.

There may be times when our future pastors invite you to share their ministry with them. When they invite you, we will be most delighted to welcome you.

We expect to grow and change because of the roots you have planted and the confidence we have gained while you were here.

Because of your ministry with us, we know the value of a pastor's presence . . . and so we will be replacing you, just as you will be replacing someone else.

We will be encouraged and cheered by reports of your ministry elsewhere, as we trust you will be by reports of our continued ministry here.[15]

The evening might conclude with each congregation member who wished giving the pastor and his family a personally written letter. The letter, written at home before the reception, could recall ways in which the pastor and his family have personally ministered to that person. It could express whatever other thoughts the person cares to include. The letters could be given to the pastor and his family by each person individually or could be gathered and placed in a "Memory Book." This type of farewell reception would, I believe, have a significant impact in facilitating the process of letting go.

Congregational members often request that a former pastor conduct weddings, funerals, or baptisms either during the interim period or during the early tenure of a new pastor (an indication that they have not fully said good-bye to their former pastor as pastor). Sometimes former pastors have agreed to do this without consulting with the new pastor or have had the congregational member request permission from the new pastor to do this.

The problem is that this practice retards the congregation's acceptance of their new pastor and may increase comparisons between the new pastor and the former one. For that reason some writers and denominational leaders have said that it should be considered unethical for a former pastor to accept such requests.[16] The problem is particularly acute if the former pastor stays within the same town or, in an even more extreme situation, retires from active ministry and remains in the congregation.

One church endeavored to affirm that the former pastor's good-bye really meant an end to his pastoral ministry in the congregation by publishing a Letter of Understanding and distributing it to all members. The letter, in adapted form, stated,

1. The pastor's resignation, effective ———, signifies his understanding that all of his pastoral and administrative duties of this congregation are terminated as of that date. He affirms that he is terminating these responsibilities willingly and not because of any coercion, believing that it is in the best interests of this congregation for him to do so.

2. It is further mutually understood that this applies also to the interim period before another pastor is called, since the congregation need some time and space between pastors to discover who they are now, where they want to go, and with what new leadership. It is agreed that the church board will make provision for other interim pastoral ministry to the congregation.

3. The former pastor agrees that he will not officiate or assist at any baptism, wedding, or funeral in this congregation but may attend as a worshiper on occasion. He may exercise his ministry in other congregations as invited. The purpose of discontinuing ministry to this congregation is to prevent divided loyalties in the congregation and pressures on the former or future pastors or interim pastors.

4. The former pastor agrees further that if attending this church in the future, it will be as a worshiper and participant, unless specifically requested by the present pastor. He also agrees that he will neither say nor listen to any uncomplimentary or critical remarks about the interim or future pastoral staff.

5. The former pastor will not attempt to influence the direction of the church in any manner. Congregational members should make their thoughts and preferences known to the interim or future pastors rather than to him.

6. The former pastor will remove his personal possessions by ——— and will return his keys, files, and other church-related items to the chairman of the board at that time.[17]

How much time should elapse between the last Sunday the departing pastor preaches and the installation of a new pastor? Richard Kirk recommends that there should be an intervening period of at least three months from the last Sunday of the departing pastor to the first service of the new pastor: "People simply need some time to let go of one pastor before they are ready really to enter a relationship with another."[18]

For some churches the processes the judicatory requires them to go through or the processes the PNC itself chooses to use virtually guarantee an interim of three months. There probably are some benefits in having an interim of at least three months between pastors. For one thing, the grieving process is probably not complete for most congregational members at the outgoing pastor's last service. An interim period allows this process to be concluded.

Another factor is that most of us, at an unconscious if not conscious level, feel it is a betrayal of our love for a person if we emotionally replace him too quickly with another person. And it probably hastens the acceptance of a new pastor if there has been a long-enough lapse between pastors that the congregation is beginning to feel "hungry," or ready for, a new permanent pastor.

9. Decide on Pulpit Supply or an Interim Pastor.

Either the board or the PNC must decide whether to contract with ministers Sunday by Sunday to lead the worship services (pulpit supply) or whether to hire an interim pastor to be responsible for this task until they select a new permanent pastor. If they choose to hire an interim pastor, they need to determine whether this appointment should be full-time or part-time.

The consensus is that the interim pastor is the preferred of these two options when available. Listed below are some advantages of an interim pastor over pulpit supply:

- It helps to reduce pressure on the PNC to "rush and get a pastor."
- It gives continuity to the preaching ministry.
- It relieves the church from having to search for a supply pastor week by week.
- It provides someone to fill the leadership gap left by the former pastor, which can stabilize the church.

- An interim pastor can give support and encouragement to the total program of the local church.
- The church can better identify with the role of the undershepherd by having the same person present week after week.
- The interim pastor will have a more sustained knowledge of the needs of the congregation than a different supply preacher each week.
- The interim pastor can try to address areas that need healing in the church through sermons, individual contacts, and meetings with various groups.
- The interim pastor reduces the parade of different speakers the congregation must listen to during the selection process.
- He can serve as a "spiritual bridge" to help transfer affection from one pastor to another. That is, people will think of their interim experience as Pastor X, followed by Interim Pastor Y, then Pastor Z. With a supply situation, people remember Pastor X, followed by a nameless and confusing sequence of supply ministers, then Pastor Z.[19]

Several writers and denominational leaders suggest that the board or the PNC contract with a potential interim to serve as a supply minister for a few services. Then if they believe this person could adequately meet the needs of the church, contract with him to become the interim pastor.

Loren Mead suggests that three types of congregations always need a trained interim:

(a) congregations that have just passed through exceptional crises or conflict with the previous pastor, (b) congregations in which the previous pastorate was particularly long—twelve to fifteen years or more, and (c) large congregations with multiple staff arrangements.[20]

Congregational members of large churches with multiple staff arrangements may sometimes be tempted to designate the associate pastor as the interim for economy. Denominational leaders and church consultants who have written about this issue unanimously agree that this is not a fair thing to do to the pastoral staff. If the associate pastor becomes the acting pastor during the interim, there may be an uncomfortable transition when the congregation selects a new senior pastor, and the church may needlessly lose a gifted associate. The associate may not receive the respect and cooperation from his former colleagues that a new interim pastor would receive. Finally, the PNC may want to consider the associate as a pastoral candidate, something they cannot do if church rules bar an interim from becoming a candidate. Thus, although there may be a temptation to save money by temporarily appointing an associate as the interim pastor, these decisions often cost more than they save.

10. The PNC and/or the Board Should Decide Whether There Are Psychological Issues Concerning the Pastorate that Need to Be Dealt with During the Interim Period.

The Presbyterian and Episcopalian denominations have taken the lead in developing methods for dealing with emotional or psychological "unfinished business" from a former pastorate. Although churches outside these two denominations rarely use these methods, pastors and judicatory leaders of every denomination said two things:

1. Failure to deal with these issues can hinder and sometimes destroy the effectiveness of a subsequent pastor.
2. Churches don't do a very good job of identifying and dealing with these kinds of problems. We sweep them under the rug and hope they'll go away by themselves.

Theologically trained pastors and pastor-overseers, not psychologists and psychiatrists, made those statements. Persons in theologically conservative denominations said them just as strongly as persons in more liberal denominations. Therefore, whatever our theological persuasion, we all have a mandate: *if we want to be fair to our next pastor, we must deal with unhealthy or unrealistic expectations of pastors, we must deal with unbiblical behavior patterns toward pastors, and we also must deal with any "unfinished business" left over from specific relationships with our last few pastors.*[21]

Several sociocultural factors probably affect how we relate to our pastors.[22] One is the current wave of consumerism. Consumers are no longer willing to acquiesce to what they consider unacceptable. Much of this outspokenness is good. However, we may fail to recognize there is a difference between assertively protesting unsatisfactory merchandise and attacking what we consider less-than-excellent performance in a pastor. Throughout Scripture there is the exhortation to show respect for the person God has called to be our spiritual leader simply because he is God's anointed one.

Another sociocultural factor is the "winning coach" mentality. If the church isn't growing numerically, or winning, get rid of the leader, and find another one. Related to this factor is the lack of relationship commitment. Thirty years ago a husband and a wife often stayed together, even through times when they weren't meeting each other's needs well, because they had made a promise to each other. Today many people aren't willing to continue in a relationship unless it is meeting their needs *in the present*. If it's failing to do that, we become angry and fight over any number of things. We often use that state of affairs to justify leaving the relationship (or forcing the other person to leave). We could use conflict as a catalyst for change—examining why we're dissatisfied and trying to make changes so the relationship is mutually satisfying again. Instead, we accept the culturally accepted belief that the best thing to do in such a situation is to discard the relationship.

Consumerism, the "winning coach" mentality, and lack of relationship commitment are affecting how we relate to our pastors. If the Old and New Testaments have anything to say to us in this regard, it's that we are to relate respectfully to our

God-given leaders. Except for immorality or theological heresy, there is no scriptural precedent for "firing" a pastor or for making things so uncomfortable for him that he resigns. On the other hand, there are biblical examples of people respectfully approaching their spiritual leader, telling him something was bothering them, and using that dissatisfaction as a catalyst for improving a relationship or situation (e.g., Zelophehad's daughters in Num. 27:1-11; the development of the office of deacon in Acts 6:1-7).

Failure to address these issues can result in the next pastor's entering an almost impossible situation. For example, in one large church the former senior pastor had been there more than twenty years. During that time he had gradually became an autocrat (an intelligent and primarily benevolent autocrat, but an autocrat nevertheless). When this pastor resigned, the deacons used the opportunity to act out their anger at their former pastor. They rewrote the church constitution, taking every bit of authority and power from the pastor's position and transferring it to the deacon board.

When the new pastor arrived at the church, he eventually learned of the changes made by the deacon board. Although a gifted pastor, he and the deacons fought over this issue and others for a year and a half, at which time he resigned with much bitterness and anger on both sides. This is only one of many possible examples illustrating that *when we don't talk out problematic issues, we are likely to act them out,* and our angry reactions may carry us to just as unbiblical extremes as the behavior to which we are reacting.

Other reasons exist for examining our behavior in this regard. First, several arguments indicate that long pastorates are more healthy than short ones for churches as a whole and for the individuals involved. John Fletcher wrote a book based on interviews he conducted with many laypersons. He concluded that "effective pastoral relationships are only built after some years of give and take as both pastor and congregation test each other's ability to be real, to care, and to believe."[23]

Second, any organization, secular or religious, going

through a change of leaders enters a period of destabilization.[24] It takes considerable time for a new leader to settle in and build a working team. These transition periods are usually times of reduced performance for the organization and increased vulnerability to outside forces. Thus, too frequent pastoral changes cause too much destabilization in a church.

Thomas Gilmore, writing about the fact that leaders in business frequently remain with one company less than three years, identified a third problem with short tenures for leaders:

> As people experience a succession of leaders, none of whom serves long enough to see a set of ideas through to realization, they find it difficult to have an intelligent sense of their institutional history. One of the most damaging results is the cynical belief that leaders can no longer make a difference. . . .
>
> Paradoxically, by withholding their commitment in such a situation, people create conditions that may make the relationship fail. A "wait and see" stance inadvertently becomes subversive, creating yet another failure to deepen the cynicism.[25]

The failure to deal with congregational issues that may result in short pastoral tenures places an awful emotional burden on pastors and their families. As a Christian psychologist, I sometimes counsel with pastors and their wives, and I frequently hear about their ministry in various churches. Some couples have suffered excruciating pain as they have given their very best to serve the church and have experienced rejection after rejection. Madalyn Murray O'Hair is credited as saying, "The Christian church is the only army in the world that shoots its wounded."

For these reasons I think it is crucial that we follow the lead of some denominations in our midst. During every pastoral change we should ask ourselves, Are there emotional issues related to the pastorate that need to be dealt with before bringing in a new pastor? If our church has had a series of short pastorates, some confrontation within the church body may be required. If a pastor has left under negative spiritual circumstances (allegations of impropriety in some area), some healing within the congregation is probably needed.

Denominations experimenting in this area often have someone from the judicatory interview members of the church in individual sessions for two days. The consultant promises confidentiality to individuals for what they say; the ideas and perspectives may be shared by the consultant, but the source is not identified. The consultant prepares a report of his findings and the suggestions for resolving the situation. He shares this report with the pastor and appropriate members of the congregation (sometimes just the board rather than the whole congregation).

One judicatory member said he frequently finds that congregations that have chronic problems getting along with their pastors suffer from one of two problems: they have lost a vision of what they are to be about, or they have one or more divisive persons within the congregation. If the former situation is true, he leads a seminar he designed to help them develop a stronger sense of mission for their church. If he finds that one or more divisive persons are causing much of the conflict, he, with the consent of the pastor and the church, leads a one-day workshop based on the book *Antagonists in the Church* by Kenneth Haugk.* If he finds the problems stem from other sources, he attempts to discover other educational programs or action plans to suit the particular situation. Probably many congregations could benefit from workshops related to communication, conflict resolution, unrealistic expectations, and handling differences. This consultant indicated that he has had positive responses to the workshops he has developed to help deal with congregational trouble spots.

These kinds of issues can be addressed in several ways. For example, a trained judicatory member may be a consultant

---

*I would recommend that every pastor and layperson read this excellent book.

to the church. Sometimes a trained consultant who is not part of a judicatory can be helpful, particularly if there is an uneasy relationship between the pastor or the congregation and the judicatory. An experienced interim pastor can sometimes address issues effectively. Within the Presbyterian Church (U.S.A.) there is now a specialization for professional interim pastors. These pastors have training in how to lead a church while it is between pastors and how to serve as a "lightning rod," dealing with unresolved issues from the last pastorate so they do not damage the ministry of the next permanent pastor. In another ten years we will undoubtedly know much more about how to deal with such issues, but even without definitive knowledge now, we can make a start.

An interim pastor or a judicatory probably will not try to deal with problematic issues unless asked by the board to do so. Therefore, the board should assess whether there are issues that need to be addressed. If there are, they should ask for help from the judicatory or the interim pastor or both. Sometimes the board or certain members of the board may be the source of the problem. In that event it may fall to the PNC to take the initiative in asking that the issues be addressed. This initiative could very appropriately come from the PNC as a result of the self-study they conduct.

11. Decide the Nature and Role of the Interim Pastor. Find Him and Empower Him to Fulfill that Role.

When people speak of an interim pastor, they may have more than one definition in mind. Traditionally the interim pastor preaches until the church finds a new pastor, and he tries to keep attendance and offerings from falling off too sharply during that period.

In the last fifteen years we have seen the development of a new phenomenon—the professional interim pastor. This person can perform all the normal pastoral duties of leading worship, visiting the sick and caring for the dying, performing marriages, providing counseling, seeing that committees are appointed and meet, and supporting and guiding the educational programs of the church.

In addition, the professional interim pastor has received training in how to help churches with the developmental tasks they must do if they are to be optimally prepared to receive a new pastor. It may include special training in how to overcome splits within the church body. It may include training in how to start the process of healing if an unhealthy pastoral situation preceded him. It without doubt included training in how to help a congregation say good-bye to a former pastor so they're ready to say hello to a new one.

Most interim pastors are peacemakers rather than prophets (i.e., confronters of wrongdoing). Sometimes an organization needs a "turnaround leader"—someone who can make drastic but needed changes to save an organization.

What all this means is that there are various kinds of interim pastors: traditional interims, interims with specialized training, interims who are primarily peacemakers, prophetic interims, and interims who can act as "turnaround" leaders if necessary. A congregation ought to know what their choices are. They then can choose the kind of interim that they need most. The church should empower the interim to fulfill the role for which they are calling him.

Giving a person responsibilities without giving him the authority to fulfill those responsibilities sets him up for frustration and failure. For example, if a church is in serious financial trouble, the interim must be given the authority to see all church books. He may need the authority to modify job descriptions and to make or recommend necessary personnel and program changes.

The board or the PNC should ask these questions of themselves: Do we want a traditional interim pastor, or do we want someone with specialized interim training? Which areas do we want him to deal with, and which areas do we want him to leave for others? Do we want a peacemaker interim, or do we need more of a prophet? Do we need someone to make drastic but necessary changes for the church to continue its existence? By defining the needs of the church more concretely, the board or the PNC increase the chance of finding an interim who will meet those needs.

Potential interim pastors can be found in the ranks of college and seminary teachers, denominational employees, and retired pastors. Those with specialized interim training may be located through your denominational judicatory or through the Alban Institute. However, don't approach anyone about employment until you've also considered the next step.

12. Divide and Delegate Pastoral Responsibilities.

At this point whoever is responsible for hiring the interim pastor should review the pastor's job description. The most essential pastoral responsibilities should be divided and delegated among paid staff and lay congregational workers. Again various choices can be made. Some churches, accustomed to having paid staff do much of the church work, may choose to have a full-time interim who will do most of what the former senior pastor did. Other churches, most notably rural churches, may be accustomed to having laypersons do a significant amount of work rather than hiring it done and so may choose to continue this practice. Once the church leaders decide what the interim pastor will be asked to do, a contract should be drawn up outlining his responsibilities, and he should be paid accordingly. It may be wise to include in the contract a statement that it will be reviewed every sixty days so that any needed changes may be made and the church may choose someone else if an interim is not working out satisfactorily.

13. Board: Develop a Worship Program that Keeps the Congregation Interested and Involved.

Concerning a worship program, Robert Dingman offers these excellent suggestions:

Schedule special events to show that the vitality of your church didn't leave with your former pastor. This is a great time for inviting "name" preachers, gifted teachers, special musical talent and seminar leaders to minister to various parts of the congregation. If you can energize your choir to a higher performance level, that in itself provides a weekly reminder that the church is healthy and God did not leave with the departed pastor.[26]

Although many people panic when their pastor leaves, fearing a catastrophe for their church, the objective evidence is far from bleak. Being without a pastor for a time actually has several advantages: "Members are more likely to feel personally responsible for the work of the church. Members are usually less demanding of perfection. Members can better appreciate the work of the new pastor for having done some of it before he came."[27]

One denominational survey found that in four out of ten churches the members believed that the work of their church suffered while it was without a pastor. But in five out of ten churches the members believed it stayed about the same in attendance, offering, and general spirit. In one out of ten churches the congregation thought it actually improved during the pastorless period.[28] There is no need for doom and gloom about the pastorless period. With effort from the congregation, a capable interim, and associate staff, the church can provide quality worship and growth experiences during the transition between pastors.

14. Board: Decide the Employment Status of Your Associate Staff and Discuss That with Them.

The transition between pastors is a time of great uncertainty for associate staff members. They often have insecurity about their jobs once the congregation selects a new pastor. This anxiety can keep them from focusing their attention on their work when the church needs them to be giving their very best.

In my interviews with denominational leaders, senior pastors, and interim pastors, I asked, "Do you think all associate staff should be expected to resign at the time a new pastor is selected?" Surprisingly, only one in five said, "Yes"; the remaining four out of five said, "No."* These were the reasons pastors and denominational leaders gave for saying no:

- It destroys the continuity of a church's ministry if all the pastors leave.
- It is unfair to associates and their families because of the time and expense involved in relocating.
- Often the congregation has deep and meaningful ties of affection to the associates.
- Often associates have much helpful information about the congregation that they can share with the incoming pastor.
- An incoming pastor's need to have everyone's resignation is a measure of his insecurity.
- The associates can provide continuity while the congregation adjusts to the new pastor's style.
- Some associates have had excellent ministries for several years. Automatically accepting their resignations will cause upheaval and anger in the congregation.
- Each associate should be hired or kept on individual merit. The decision to keep an associate should be based on the ability to serve and to cooperate with the new senior pastor.

Persons interviewed said that exceptional situations would make it necessary to ask for all associates' resignations. Two examples would be a staff that had a history of undermining senior pastors and a staff that had a need to significantly change the way the entire pastoral staff was operating.

In this matter each board must consult its church constitution (a few require that all associates resign at the time a church selects a new senior pastor). It also will need to consider the work quality of the associate staff presently at the church.

*The actual percentages were 22 percent "yes," 78 percent "no."

Various people have made the following suggestions with regard to mandatory resignations:

1. If a staff member is clearly doing unacceptable work, the board should tell him or her that they would like the resignation before or when the church calls a new pastor. This procedure prevents the new pastor from having a staff dismissal as one of his first official acts.

2. If a staff member is doing good work, the board should tell him so and also explain that whether he continues at the church after the selection of a new pastor will be up to him and the new pastor. The board and the PNC will tell the incoming pastor that in their eyes, this person has been an effective minister, and they hope that the senior pastor and this staff member can work cooperatively together. If after working together for a time the associate decides not to stay, the church will provide some transition time (specify how long) while he finds another place of ministry. (Make certain to have this understanding approved, preferably in writing, with whatever board in your church needs to approve such matters.)

3. When the committee interviews a pastoral candidate, he can be asked about his beliefs on whether all associates' resignations should automatically be expected and accepted. His answer, and his reasons for it, can be part of the basis on which the PNC decides whether to recommend him to the board and the congregation.

15. Identify Activities of the PNC.

The following activities are discussed in detail in the coming chapters. They are mentioned briefly here to give you an overview of the processes the PNC will be going through.

A. Develop a pastor profile. Use scriptural criteria, and translate the organizational needs identified in your self-study into leadership qualities desired in your next pastor. Include congregational input.

B. Ask for feedback on your self-study and pastor profile from your judicatory and board.

C. Identify the methods you will use to find potential applicants. Include recommendations from your congregation.

D. Develop statements and questions you will use when talking with referral sources and attempting to elicit names of potential applicants from them. Develop written materials to send to referral resources you think would respond better to written requests. (Referral resources are people you contact who may be good sources of names of potential applicants. They are generally not applicants themselves.)

E. Develop materials you will send to potential applicants (this will include basic information about your church and a Pastor's Information Form).

F. Send these materials to everyone who is identified by your referral resources or your congregation or who requests information after having learned of your pastoral vacancy through another means.

G. Send a personalized form letter to individuals who send in an application, letting them know about the process you will be using, when they may expect to hear from you again, and any pieces that are lacking from their applications.

H. Review the initial applications according to the criteria you have developed. Do not listen to audiotapes of sermons at this point. Eliminate those who clearly do not meet your criteria. If you still have many candidates left after your first round of eliminations, write a nonacceptance letter to those no longer being considered so that you do not keep them waiting unnecessarily.

I. Interview by telephone the references of the remaining candidates. Have three committee members listen to both audiotapes sent by each applicant and rate them independently. Have a second round of eliminations based on feedback from references and responses to audiotapes. Reduce your candidate pool to the top five or six applicants.

J. Prepare questions that you will ask all candidates and identify which committee members will ask each set of questions. Decide the order that various committee members will go in. Your interview will seem to the applicant to be more organized if each person takes one topic and asks all the questions related to that topic. Then that person and others can ask follow-up questions related to the topic that they compose at the moment in response to the applicant's answers. Only after one committee member has completed a line of questions should the next member begin a new topic.

Before beginning the interview with each applicant, identify questions that you may have for the applicant that you are not asking all candidates. Designate one or more persons to ask those questions.

K. Call those pastors you are still considering and let them know that the committee would like to interview them and their spouses in person. If they live a considerable distance from your church, the interview can be done by conference telephone. Confirm whether they still wish to be considered (some may have had situational changes since sending in an application). If they still wish to be considered, tell them you will send them a copy of your self-study so they can learn more about the church. If some of the information is less than flattering to your church, ask them to consider the self-study confidential, to be read and discussed only with the spouse. Schedule a personal or telephone interview, and send the self-study.

L. From these interviews identify your strongest candidates. If you feel it is necessary, visit the candidates in their home churches during a worship service to make your final decision. If you feel this step is unnecessary, present your strongest candidate to the board. Summarize that candidate's background, training, and experience and why you believe the person would make a good pastor for your church.

M. Once approved by the board (and your judicatory if that is necessary), invite your strongest candidate to come to your church, preferably for five days (Wednesday through Sunday). Arrange for him to meet in small groups with as many people from the church as is realistic. Use a semicontrolled agenda (more about this in a later chapter).

N. Have the congregation vote either that Sunday or the following one. If the vote is positive, extend a call. If not, recycle to Step L, and repeat until a new pastor is found.

O. Send nonacceptance letters to the remainder of the applicants.

P. Send thank-you letters to those who have been helpful in your search process.

Q. Destroy personal information of candidates that was collected during the search process.

R. Celebrate!

S. Designate at least one person from your committee (preferably the chair) to stay in touch with your new pastor and provide practical help during his move to the church and for the first three months in his new position. This person should help the new pastor develop strong, positive relationships with denominational leaders, neighboring clergypersons, congregational leaders, and members.

A chart of these suggested steps, breaking them down into the ones for the board and the ones for the PNC, is found in Appendix B. This chart will help you understand the next steps that need to be taken as you go through the process.

See Appendix C for a sample charter and charge to a PNC.

Creating a
Pastor Profile and Beyond

Some Preliminary Considerations

Develop Concrete Expectations

Robert Mager tells a fable that illustrates the importance of becoming specific when we are searching for a candidate for any position:

> Once upon a time in the land of Fuzz, King Aling called in his cousin Ding and commanded, "Go ye out into all of Fuzzland and find me the goodest of men, whom I shall reward for his goodness."
>
> "But how will I know one when I see one?" asked the Fuzzy.
>
> "Why, he will be *sincere*," scoffed the king, and whacked off a leg for his impertinence.
>
> So, the Fuzzy limped out to find a good man. But soon he returned, confused and empty-handed.
>
> "But how will I know one when I see one?" he asked again.
>
> "Why, he will be *dedicated*," grumbled the king, and whacked off another leg for his impertinence.
>
> So the Fuzzy hobbled away once more to look for the goodest of men. But again he returned, confused and empty-handed.

"But how will I know one when I see one?" he pleaded.

"Why, he will have *internalized his growing awareness,*" fumed the king, and whacked off another leg for his impertinence.

So the Fuzzy, now on his last leg, hopped out to continue his search. In time, he returned with the wisest, most sincere and dedicated Fuzzy in all of Fuzzland, and stood him before the king.

"Why, this man won't do at all," roared the king. "He is much too thin to suit me." Whereupon, he whacked off the last leg of the Fuzzy, who fell to the floor with a squishy thump.

The moral of this fable is that . . . *if you can't tell one when you see one, you may wind up without a leg to stand on.*[1]

Mager goes on to point out that we are likely to achieve our goals in direct proportion to how concretely (or specifically) wc identify them. Applying his fable to the goal of this book, we are likely to choose a pastor who can effectively lead us in the next five to ten years of our church's growth only to the degree that we have become specific about the qualities our next pastor needs.

Robert Dingman makes the following excellent comments:

Most relationships between a leader and his followers that go sour do so because of expectations that went unfulfilled. And the tragedy is that, in most cases, those expectations were never clearly expressed by the parties involved. Careful exploration before the hiring takes place can usually avoid the disastrous results of a failed relationship.[2]

Thus, our search is likely to be successful and our relationship with our future pastor more satisfying to the degree that we develop a concrete, specific picture of the characteristics we want our new pastor to have (i.e., a pastor profile).

Avoid Hypercriticalness

Sometimes a church has had a negative experience with a previous pastor. Or the members may have developed a habit of being hypercritical of their pastors. Either can result in hypercriticalness on the PNC. Elliot Brack, a newspaper editor in metropolitan Atlanta, must have served on one such committee. Here is his description of the PNC on which he served:

> When it comes to picking its leaders, many American churches may be operating back in Neanderthal days. Compared with modern business practices, for most Protestant churches, picking a new pastor is an abomination. . . .
> The minister (almost on trial) must perform. A bad performance and he (or she these days) is doomed to seek another "call."
> But even a good pulpit performance doesn't hold water for the Pulpit Committee. They have to think about it, you see, going over in detail the performance of the poor soul before them. They analyze his every joke, his manner, even the way he sings, or greets people. Was his handshake firm enough? Was it too firm? Any little flaw, and presto! The committee can't reach a consensus. . . . Let's consider someone else. . . .
> Wear the wrong color suit, and you're out. Be a little too funny, and the committee questions the sincerity. Be too serious, and they question if you will be able to relate to people.[3]

If you recognize that your committee is hypercritical, make sure to address this issue. Your committee, or perhaps the whole church, needs to understand what is causing the hypercriticalness and make changes at that level before proceeding with the pastoral search.

Encourage Input from the Entire PNC

A good way to build morale and cohesion in the PNC is to provide a group setting where everyone feels included in the discussion process. Here are some ways to encourage participation from everyone on the PNC:

An effective discussion usually occurs when:	An effective discussion usually does not occur when:
1. People feel they have an opportunity to contribute.	One or two people dominate group time.
2. People feel they have the right to choose how they are going to share.	People feel pressured to share when they are not ready or comfortable doing so.
3. Every person feels that others value his or her perspectives, even when they disagree.	People ridicule or never affirm (ignore) the ideas of others.
4. The group develops new insights or perspectives.	The group reiterates the same perspectives it already held.
5. The group comes prepared to work, with necessary data or preparation done beforehand.	The group comes unprepared and pools its ignorance.
6. The group stays on one topic until it finds some sort of closure before moving on to another.	The group leader allows the discussion to wander from one topic to another without achieving closure.
7. The leader directs the discussion so that it remains focused on meaningful, answerable issues.	The leader allows discussion to digress to unanswerable questions or issues of questionable relevance.
8. People feel free to reach their own conclusions and to hold differing opinions.	People feel pressured to agree with the group consensus.
9. Group members show an interest in the ideas of others. Dialogue occurs.	Group members try to impose their ideas onto others. Monologues and minilectures occur.

An effective discussion usually occurs when:	An effective discussion usually does not occur when:
10. Group members show respect for one another by being on time, being attentive, and not causing distractions.	Group members cause distractions and act uninterested when others speak.
11. People express their ideas tentatively.	People express their ideas dogmatically.
12. There is freedom to be "in process" with one's ideas and to express ideas imperfectly.	Members criticize "in-process" ideas rather than build upon them.
13. Group atmosphere remains casual, friendly, and involved.	Group atmosphere becomes marked by tension, anger, or indifference.

Recognize This Time Can Be One of Spiritual Growth

Alban consultant Loren Mead tells the story of an Episcopalian friend who called him in distress. The friend's rector had just resigned, and the vestry had asked him to be part of the PNC. Though not insensitive to his friend's distress, Mead related that he felt very differently about his friend and that church's future than did his friend. These were Mead's thoughts:

I knew they were potentially off to discover a new world of ministry and mission. They were entering a time—a year or a year and a half—in which they would have to rethink and reevaluate who they were, what they thought they were supposed to be up to, what they valued and cared about. I knew that if they followed the path of literally hundreds of other congregations who go through the process of pastoral change every year, they would be forced to push themselves up against their basic commitments and their religious heritage, and they would have to choose once again whether to take them seriously or not. They would have to make that commitment anew, for themselves, and not rely on what former generations had stood for or valued. It would give them a new chance to "own" what the church is all about.[4]

Avoid Expectations for the Future Pastor That Are Self-Destructive or Family Destructive

It's very easy to set expectations for pastors that cause personal burnout or that damage their family and marital life. Pastors have a hard time standing against the collective congregational expectations that are almost invariably present. This short article points out some of these expectations, as seen through the eyes of one parishioner.

A Case of Unprofessional Conduct

I don't know what we're going to do about Pastor Cooper. He didn't attend the meeting to choose paint for the new fellowship hall. Said he was taking his son to the movies. Said we could choose the right color without him. Can you imagine? And he didn't come to the missions committee meeting! His son had a band concert at school that night and he went there instead. Well, sure he's a neat kid. He wants to be a minister like his father, I know, but there ought to be priorities, don't you think?

OK, so a man has to be with his family. But how about the time he didn't come to the young singles bowling banquet? He'd been visiting hospital patients all day and said he was just too tired. Too tired! When the minister comes to something, that means it's important. I guess the bowling banquet wasn't important. But he never misses the evangelism meetings, does he? He's never too tired for them!

You remember the special Golden Agers program we planned in October? Pastor Cooper missed it! He took Diane out to dinner. To dinner yet! Well, sure, it was their wedding anniversary, but they could have gone another night. As long as they celebrated, what difference does it make which night? Diane shouldn't be so sentimental. Bill and I haven't celebrated our anniversary for years, and we're still together, aren't we?

Another thing that bugs me. He won't make Diane work in the church. When we needed Sunday school teachers we thought he'd tell her to sign up for the training class, but he didn't. I know she heads up Pioneer Girls but that just makes her more qualified to teach Sunday school.

One thing for certain, Pastor Cooper isn't like Pastor Ormstead.

I miss him a lot. He was so—*available*. Any time the church was open, he'd be there. You could call him day or night and he'd come.

He was in everything, remember? Out every night of the week. And our church really grew under his ministry, you've got to admit that. It was a real shame he had to resign, but after the divorce we couldn't very well keep him on. You know how it is.[5]

Data to Consider When Developing a Pastor Profile

I believe we should examine three basic areas when developing qualities for a pastor profile. First would be the biblical references in 1 Timothy 3 and Titus 1 that give us qualities required in persons who would be pastors. Second would be psychological studies of the qualities it takes to be a good leader. Third is a self-study. By completing a self-study, a congregation will have a clearer idea of its present and future needs. These needs can then be translated into qualities held by the congregation's leader, the pastor, to meet those needs most effectively.

Biblical Qualities

First Timothy 3:1–7 and Titus 1:5–9 give the prerequisite biblical qualities for anyone desiring to be a pastor. The King

James Version translated this office as that of "bishop," but a consensus among Protestant commentators is that this passage describes the office of pastor of a local congregation.*

The characteristics found in the two texts noted can be organized into twelve groupings:[6]

1. *Personal character above reproach from within and without the church. Anepileptos,* the word translated "blameless" or "above reproach" in 1 Timothy 3:2, means not only of good report but deservedly so.[7] N. J. D. White describes it as "one against whom it is impossible to bring any charge of wrong doing such as could stand impartial examination."[8] According to Edmond Hiebert, Titus 1:6 states that a pastor must have "an irreproachable reputation in the community" and within the church.[9]

2. *Thoughtful, dignified, and self-controlled. Kosmios* means "orderly, respectable, honorable, and modest." *Sophron* means "in control of his mind and emotions so that he can act rationally and discreetly." *Egkrates* (see Titus 1:8) means "having the inner strength that enables him to control his bodily appetites and passions."[10] A pastor should be a person of proven thoughtfulness, dignity, and self-discipline.

3. *Not a neophyte. Neophytos* means one recently baptized or "newly planted." Too rapid promotion of a young Christian can easily lead to excessive pride (see 1 Tim. 3:6).[11] Natural abilities notwithstanding, a recent convert should not be promoted to the position of pastor.

4. *Not a drunkard. Me paroinos* means "not one who sits long at his wine" or "not one who lingers with the cup."[12] Therefore, this phrase means someone who is temperate

---

*The word *episkopos* (overseers) is generally believed to be used for the same group as *presbuteros* (elders). In the early church apparently several men in each congregation were designated overseers or elders. Some were teaching elders, and others were ruling elders. The teaching elder eventually developed into the position we now call pastor. These qualifications apply to all who would be chosen to be either ruling or teaching elders and therefore legitimately are applied to persons who would be pastors.

(*nephalios*), or who does not use alcohol (and in this day, drugs) excessively. *Substance abuse* and *substance addiction* would be the contemporary technical terms that indicate this disqualification.

5. *Not violent, quick-tempered, quarrelsome, arrogant, or overbearing. Me plektes, amachos, orgilon, authades. Me plekten* means "not a striker," not one who becomes involved in drunken brawls, not one who is ready to assail an opponent with fists or verbal behavior. *Me amachon* means "not quarrelsome or contentious, abstaining from fighting, noncombative."

Titus 1:7 adds two further disqualifications. *Orgilon* means "quick-tempered," that is, "yielding readily to anger."[13] *Authades* means not "overbearing," that is, "arrogantly disregarding the interests of others in order to please oneself."[14]

6. *Not a lover of money or a pursuer of dishonest gain. Aphilarguros* refers to someone who is a lover of money (see 1 Tim. 3:3). *Aischrokerde* refers to someone who pursues dishonest gain (see Titus 1:7). Pastors have a legitimate right to be concerned about providing for the needs of the family and therefore have the same rights as all wage earners to be recompensed fairly for their work, but money should never be their motivation for ministry. The wage scales of most churches effectively deter from the pastorate most people whose motivation for ministry would be money.

7. *Gentle in his dealings with men (epieikes).* E. K. Simpson says, "*Epieikes* defies exact translation. . . . *Gracious, kindly, forbearing, considerate, magnanimous, genial* all approximate to its idea."[15]

8. *Upright and holy in his life before God.* Edmond Hiebert describes *dikaios* as "upright, conforming his conduct to right standards." *Hosios* denotes his personal piety, "an inner attitude of conforming to what is felt to be pleasing to God and consistent with religious practices."[16]

9. *Loves what is good. Philagothos* (see Titus 1:8) means that the potential pastor must be "an ally and zealous supporter of the good, including men and deeds and things."[17]

10. *Faithful monogamy, with a well-ordered home and disciplined children.* Highly respected Greek scholar A. T. Robertson says that *mias gunaikos andra* refers to "one [wife] at a time, clearly."[18] Ralph Earle summarizes the most common view accepted by Protestant theologians in the following way:

> Some have interpreted this as meaning "married only once." By the end of the second century this interpretation was being promulgated, under the influence of an asceticism that led to clerical celibacy in the Roman Catholic Church. Bernard [a leader in the early church] defends this view emphatically. He writes of the phrase here: "It excludes from ecclesiastical position those who have been married more than once." Today most commentators agree that it means monogamy—only one wife at one time—and that the overseer must be completely faithful to his wife.[19]

It is not likely that the criterion "husband of but one wife" forbids remarriage if the first wife died (see Rom. 7:2–3; 1 Cor. 7:39; 1 Tim. 5:14). It is also not likely that this verse means that a pastor had to be married: "If Paul had meant that the elder must be married, the reading would have been 'a,' not 'one,' wife. Most natural is the view that he must be the husband of only one living woman."[20] In the next section I will discuss how a PNC can handle the issue of whether a divorced person can ever be considered for pastoral leadership.

Paul devotes more space to the pastor's management of his family than to any other single criterion, so God must consider family management particularly important. First Timothy 3:4–5 reads, "He must manage his own family well and see that his children obey him with proper respect. (If anyone does not know how to manage his own family, how can he take care of God's church?)" (NIV). Titus 1:6 adds that a pastor must have children who "believe and are not open to the charge of being wild and disobedient."

The Greek word *teknon,* which Paul uses in both passages,

refers to (nonadult) children who would normally be living at home. This word is not referring to a pastor's *adult* offspring. While they are still children under their parents' care, they should have a personal faith, and the parents should use a proper combination of love and discipline so that the children are obedient and respectful. Rarely are questions regarding this area included in a pastor's applications or interviews.

11. *Hospitable.* *Philoxenos* means "loving strangers," therefore "given to hospitality." Ralph Earle helps to put this term in historical perspective:

> Christians travelling in the first century avoided the public inns with their pagan atmosphere and food that had already been offered to idols (cf. 1 Cor. 8). So they would seek out a Christian home in which to stop for the night. A valuable by-product was that believers from widely scattered areas would get to know each other, cementing lines of fellowship. So hospitality was an important Christian virtue in that day.[21]

Probably all of us recognize the importance even today of pastors who enjoy showing hospitality.

12. *An apt teacher who has matured in his knowledge of the faith, holds firm to sound doctrine and can impart it to others, and can refute those who oppose the truth.* Expositors have elaborated the Greek word *didaktikos* and the accompanying phrases in the following ways. A. T. Robertson defines it as "one qualified to teach."[22] Newport White defines it as "not merely the ability, but also the willingness, to teach."[23] W. E. Vine says, "Not merely a readiness to teach is implied, but the spiritual power to do so as the outcome of prayerful meditation in the Word of God and the practical application of its truth to oneself."[24] The pastor, then, "must hold firmly to the trustworthy message as it has been taught, so that he can encourage others by sound doctrine and refute those who oppose it (Titus 1:9 NIV)." The candidate who is unsure of the authority of God's Word or of the truthfulness of its teachings would fail to meet this criterion.

Controversial Issues

As we consider these biblical criteria, several controversies may emerge within the committee. I believe we can best handle these issues by explicitly discussing them as a committee and making a decision about each one. For some of these issues, there may be a strong consensus immediately, so little discussion will be needed. For others, more time will be necessary to reach a consensus.

Occasionally the committee may agree on a given criterion, but the congregation may be divided, perhaps strongly so. What should the committee do? Should they take an educative stance and try to shift congregational opinion? Should they withhold information that might be unacceptable to portions of the congregation (such as a candidate's divorce many years ago) because they believe the candidate would be an excellent choice?

Each committee will ultimately have to decide the wisest course to pursue. However, here are my thoughts on these general questions. First, I do not think the committee should withhold information about a candidate from the congregation because they know that some congregational members would respond negatively. The congregation almost inevitably discovers this information later. The PNC's lack of candor causes the congregation to feel betrayed, and the negative feelings can lead to termination of the pastor or to a congregational split.

Second, I do not think the PNC should try to change congregational opinions so that members will accept a candidate not presently acceptable to them. Neither the board nor the congregation has given the PNC this responsibility, and if the PNC tries to assume it, the congregation will likely respond negatively. Sometimes the committee will believe that the congregation's opinions should be changed in a certain area so that people will be receptive to a candidate they would not presently accept. In this case the area might be one in which the next pastor could bring teaching, the Sunday school might offer teaching and discussion groups, or the congregation might form an issue-oriented study group. In this way the congregation's opinions might be changed before the *next* pastoral change occurs, but probably the present committee should use criteria for their nominee that they know will be acceptable to most of the present congregation's thinking.

Third, any choice of pastor is likely to cause a few persons to leave the church. If most of the congregation would agree with certain criteria, it is probably not necessary to find criteria on which every congregational member is in agreement. The PNC should represent the general consensus of the congregation, not every opinion of individual members. Listed below are some specific questions the PNC may wish to address.

How closely does your committee want to follow the biblical criteria? Hardly any of the denominational leaders, pastors, or materials developed for screening pastors thoroughly examine each candidate on the twelve criteria discussed in the section "Biblical Qualities." And that includes several conservative denominations that usually show great concern about trying to use scriptural guidelines in all things. In the forms and interview questions suggested in the remainder of the book, I will incorporate questions pertaining to these twelve areas. If your committee does not believe that these criteria should continue to be used, these questions can be omitted.

What if the applicant has been fired from a previous pastorate? Some people believe that a pastor who has been fired must have some serious shortcomings and should not be considered seriously by the committee. A related opinion, expressed by several people I interviewed, is that inadequate pastors generally do not change.

The opposing viewpoint is that having been fired is no reason to automatically disqualify an applicant. The termination may say more about the church, or some of its members, than it does about the pastor. Everyone makes mistakes, including persons who will eventually become great leaders. Peter F.

Drucker has said, "No significant achiever makes it without a failure before 40."[25]

Sometimes a congregation and a pastor may not get along because of conflicting visions of ministry, conflicting priorities, or conflicting expectations. In a different church, where there is more compatibility between the pastor's and the congregation's visions, an effective relationship may develop.

Healthy people *do change* as a result of their mistakes. If a pastor has been fired from a previous pastorate, rather than automatically dismiss his application, a committee can find out the circumstances involved. They can ask the candidate what he has learned from the experience and ask denominational overseers their view of his ability to pastor your church. If a pattern of similar problems has recurred in two or more pastorates, and if the denominational overseer is less than optimistic that the pastor has made changes, the committee may want to bypass that applicant.

Should men and women be considered? This extremely important issue continues to generate controversy. In some congregations women will be accepted as associate pastors, youth pastors, and Christian education directors but not as senior pastors. As mentioned earlier, I do not think the PNC's role is to try to break new ground theologically. The committee should try to find candidates who will be acceptable to the broad majority of the congregation. The committee that believes the congregation needs to grow in its theological understanding of a certain topic can seek candidates who will challenge the congregation to grow.

Should candidates who have been involved in moral failure be considered? Some denominations automatically disqualify a pastor involved in moral failure from ever serving in the pastorate again. Others prescribe a certain amount of time during which the pastor must withdraw from public ministry and enter some rehabilitation process before his credentials can be restored.

Advocates for both positions can point to biblical support for their ideas. At the stricter end, advocates can point to the fact that pastors are to have blameless lives above reproach; their lives are to be examples of holy and disciplined living. Advocates for the withdrawal-and-rehabilitation approach point to the character of God—His grace—as well as to the fact that He continued to use believers, even those who made serious mistakes while believers (e.g., David, Simon Peter). They also point out that all the criteria for pastors are in the present tense. They do not require that a person have lived a sinless life but indicate the kind of life the pastoral applicant is living now. Each committee must answer this question for itself.

Should divorced applicants be considered? Those who take a stricter view refer to the fact that a pastor is to be "the husband of one wife" and "one who rules his family well" (1 Tim. 3:2, 4). Even if his wife initiated the divorce without adequate grounds for doing so, they interpret the divorce as prima facie evidence that he hadn't ruled his family well. Advocates for a less-strict view might urge looking at the circumstances that prompted the divorce. A pastor who was trying to be a good husband and father might be divorced by a wife who became infatuated with the local tennis pro. He is not responsible for, nor should he be punished for, her sinful decision. This approach would recommend understanding the circumstances surrounding a divorce and the kind of life the pastor has lived since the divorce before making a decision about whether an applicant should be considered.

Are there implicit expectations for the pastor's wife? There is probably no other area for which a congregation has more unverbalized expectations than this one—until the pastor's wife fails to meet them. Is she as free to be involved or uninvolved in church events as any other woman in the congregation, or are there extra expectations for her? If there are, it's unfair for the PNC not to discuss them with the applicant and his spouse. Then they can decide if these expectations are compatible with her personality and gifts.

Other issues will be crucial in various denominations or congregations: topics such as belief in the authority and trustworthiness of Scripture, the relationship of the pastor with the board, the relationship of the congregation with the denomination, the use of alcohol, abortion, attitudes toward homosexuality and the ordination of homosexuals, and attitudes toward the National and World Council of Churches.

Psychological Studies of What Makes a Good Leader

Leaders Versus Managers

In recent years considerable discussion has focused on the differences between leaders and managers. Although such discussions reflect the semantic differences each author chooses to give to the terms, spending a moment applying this discussion to pastors may be helpful. It could be argued that individual pastors tend to be either leaders or managers. Here are some general differences between these two:

Leader-pastors	Manager-pastors
1. Develops new visions for the congregation	Strengthens and maintains visions already there
2. Willing to take risks	Cautious about taking risks
3. Initiator of new ideas	Responds to new ideas from others
4. High emotional involvement in work	Moderate emotional involvement in work
5. Biggest risk—people will not become excited about his new vision	Biggest risk—people become bored or self-centered because not sufficiently challenged

Leaders-as-Heroes Versus Leaders-as-Developers

Another idea from the leadership literature that may be useful in the study of pastors is the conceptual movement from leader-as-hero to leader-as-developer. The leader-as-hero "rides to the rescue" when there is a problem. He gives answers. He assumes total responsibility for the success or failure of an organization. The leader-as-developer has the dual goal of getting the job done while engaging subordinates in a way that stimulates them to grow and take responsibility. He learns to have an impact without exerting total control. He learns to be helpful without having all the answers. He learns to be responsible for the organization without diminishing subordinates' sense of responsibility for their part in it.[26]

The pastor-as-developer model is healthier for leaders and subordinates than the pastor-as-hero model. The pastor-as-hero model encourages the pastor to assume an omniscience and omnipotence that only God possesses. It encourages him to be the initiator and organizer of every church activity and encourages passivity among church members, which can lead to frustration and burnout on the pastor's part. The pastor-as-developer (or pastor-as-equipper) allows a church to be more effective (because more people share the work). It results in higher morale (because more people feel useful) and, it could be argued, is more biblical (see 1 Cor. 12:12–21; Eph. 4:12).

Donald Walters has made some thoughtful comments related to these two styles of leadership. In the leader-as-hero model, the leader can easily become impressed with his self-importance. Walters says that self-importance in a leader is self-defeating. The spirit of a group reflects the spirit of its leader—if he focuses on his importance, his followers will focus on theirs. One's ego can be either a hindrance or an aid to creativity. It is an aid to creativity if its energy flow is toward the job to be done; it is a hindrance if the energy flow is inward upon oneself. Leadership is giving service, not receiving it. Leadership is not an ego game.[27]

In regard to leaders-as-developers, Walters offers the following recommendations. Work with people as they are, not as you want them to be. Work with things as they are, not as you want them to be. Be patient. Understand that it takes time to bring people to new points of view. To win loyalty, be loyal first. To win love, first give love.[28]

The Process of Leadership

The process of leadership can be conceptualized as having five sets of skills: envisioning, planning, budgeting, organizing, and controlling.[29] Let's look at each one in more detail.

John Kotter says, "Great vision emerges when a powerful mind, working long and hard on massive amounts of information, is able to see (or recognize in suggestions from others) interesting patterns and new possibilities."[30] *Envisioning* creates a vision of what should be, a vision that considers the legitimate interests of all the people involved. For a pastor, envisioning would involve developing a vision for the specific role his church can play in his community and in the world at large.

Planning involves developing a strategy for accomplishing that vision. This strategy should consider all the environmental forces and organizational factors. A pastor's vision for a church should consider the situation in the world outside his church and the ability of his congregation to address specific portions of the world's needs. Planning requires a keen mind, moderately strong analytical abilities, good judgment, and the capacity to think strategically and multidimensionally.

Budgeting is that part of the planning processes concerned with allocation of funds. In a church it requires the ability to live within our means, to use available funds in a thoughtful balance of ministry to the church body itself and its mission outside itself. It also includes the ability to explain persuasively to advocates of various programs why they may not be funded to the degree requested.

Organizing involves creating a structure that can accomplish the vision. It also involves staffing the organization with qualified people, defining clearly each person's role, providing people with adequate support resources, and delegating appropriate authority to them.

Controlling means looking constantly for deviations from the plan ("problems") and then helping the individuals involved to solve them. In the church these problems can be organizational, interpersonal, or financial. Control may occur through "review" meetings of several involved people or through a less formal meeting with the delegated head of that department.

The leader-as-developer concept requires that during the organizing and controlling stages the leader develop a highly motivated group of key people who adopt the vision as their own. They are willing to share the work and responsibility necessary to bring it to fruition. It is not the "pastor's vision" anymore; it has become their own.

Donald Walters makes two other very significant comments in this regard. He says, "Genuine leadership . . . leads people: it doesn't coerce them. It never loses sight of the most important principle governing any project involving human beings: namely, that *people are more important than things*."[31] He adds, "When people are not inspired to give of themselves, they revert naturally to thinking what they can get for themselves."[32]

Fred A. Manske, Jr., has written a book identifying the ingredients of effective leadership. He is speaking of a business relationship where subordinates are employees and not volunteers; therefore, the leader he describes can be more demanding than can a pastor who works primarily with a volunteer staff. However, his list of characteristics is relevant. According to him, an effective leader

- builds group cohesiveness and pride.
- lives by the highest standards of honesty and integrity.
- shares information openly and willingly.
- coaches to improve performance.
- insists on excellence.
- sets the example for others to follow.
- holds subordinates accountable.
- has courage.
- shows confidence in people.
- is decisive.
- has a strong sense of urgency.
- makes every minute count.
- earns the loyalty of employees [congregation members].
- is employee centered [congregation centered].
- listens to subordinates.

- is determined.
- is available and visible to his or her staff.[33]

The Self-Study

A self-study will aid the pastoral search process in three ways. First, it can be an excellent introduction to the church for applicants and candidates. Second, the PNC can translate the needs of the church that they identify during the self-study into qualities needed by their next pastor. Third, the self-study enables the committee to involve the entire congregation in the search process very early and very meaningfully. I would recommend that the entire teenage and adult congregation devote a Sunday school session to completing a Congregational Self-Study Form (see Appendix D).

A comprehensive self-study should address the following nine areas. A selective summary of this self-study can be sent to all applicants; the full self-study can be sent to the finalists.[34]

1. A General Description of the Church in its Community Context[35]

In a combination of prose and tabular form, include the following information (prose descriptions seem emotionally "warmer" and less formal than primarily numerical presentations of data; use prose descriptions when possible):

- Date of church's inception.
- Number of members, Sunday A.M. attendance, Sunday school attendance five years ago and today.
- Breakdown by age, for example, percentage of members under 20, between 20 and 34, between 35 and 49, between 50 and 64, and 65 and older.
- The career and educational levels of the congregation.
- Total annual budget and missions budget.
- Programs for children ages 12 and under.
- Programs for young people ages 13 through 21.

- Adult group organizations, including the name of the group, frequency with which group meets, and its usual attendance.
- Description of the buildings, discussion of their adequacy for present church programs, mortgage indebtedness, and monthly mortgage payments.
- A list of all salaried staff besides the pastor. Include person's name, position, and number of hours included in contract.
- Names of the last three pastors who have served the church and their dates of service. Indicate the reason the last pastor left and what he is doing now.

2. General Description of the Community

- Describe the type of community immediately surrounding the church.
- Describe the racial composition, ages, educational levels, and occupations of the community. Are any significant changes in the community's composition occurring now?
- What quality of education is available at the primary, secondary, college, and graduate levels?
- What cultural, scientific, and recreational opportunities are available within the community or within a driving distance of two hours or less?
- What medical care is available?
- What challenges is the community facing? If the community has a reputation for problems in a certain area, what is being done to try to solve those problems?

3. The History of the Church

- Identify significant dates and events.
- Give a brief description of the pastors who have served and their most important contributions if the church has a short history. If the church has a long history, do this only for selected pastors.

- If the church has had to deal with significant challenges at various times in its history, describe them and how the church has resolved them (if it has). If the church has not resolved a challenge or problem, discuss it in section five below.

4. Strengths of the Church

- Using the items that come from the Congregational Self-Study Forms (Appendix D) and the PNC's own thoughts, discuss the church's present strengths.

5. Weaknesses of the Church or Challenges Facing the Church

- Using the items that come from the Congregational Self-Study Forms and the PNC's own thoughts, discuss those areas that need to be strengthened or issues that need to be resolved.
- This section can also include theological issues about which there is controversy.
- The PNC should probably agree as a group about the level of self-disclosure to be given to all pastoral applicants. Remember that what the PNC shares at this level will undoubtedly become somewhat public knowledge. Therefore, do not give information that would be destructive if it were to reach the congregation.
- The level of self-disclosure to finalists can and should be somewhat higher. The PNC can ask finalists and their spouses to keep this information confidential—they should use it only to help them make the decision about whether they have the gifts the church needs now.

6. Challenges of the Next Five to Ten Years

- This information should come from the Congregational Self-Study Forms and the PNC's discussions.

- Some of this information will obviously be somewhat speculative. However, that should not prevent you from including it. A congregation and a PNC that have been thinking and planning for the future will favorably impress an applicant.

7. Parishioners' Thoughts on Priorities

- This information, summarized from the Congregational Self-Study Forms, will give the applicant an idea of the expectations of the congregation and whether his concept of pastoral ministry complements those expectations.
- If there is much scatter among the congregation's expectations, include this information, too. Having a congregation with conflicting expectations represents a more complex task for the pastor.
- Significant differences between the expectations of the PNC and those of the congregation should be discussed. The PNC and the board represent the leadership of the church. Sometimes the leadership and general laity have different expectations for their pastor. Not every pastor feels comfortable coming into such a situation, and applicants should be informed if this is present.

8. Qualities the Next Pastor Should Possess

- These qualities can be summarized from the PNC's discussions and the Congregational Self-Study Forms.

9. Salary and Benefits

- Salary should be expressed in general terms and as a range rather than a fixed number.
- If a church is small and cannot afford to pay a full-time pastor's salary, identify opportunities for other part-time work compatible with pastoring.
- More information on this topic will be covered in the next chapter.

Developing Assessment Methods

There are five primary ways that PNCs may assess, with a minimum of cost, the degree to which an applicant meets their criteria. **They are (1) answers to the Pastor's Information Form, (2) information from references, (3) credit check and police records check, (4) analysis of tapes of sermons, and (5) answers to a carefully prepared personal interview.**

I have listed here the qualities that God says are prerequisites for the position of pastor (one through twelve) and some of the qualities psychology recommends if one is to be an effective leader (thirteen through twenty-four). Following each quality are numbers (keyed to sources in the preceding paragraph) that indicate where you can obtain information about that particular quality for each applicant.

1. Personal character above reproach from within and without the church—2, 3.

2. Thoughtful, dignified, and self-controlled—1, 2, 3, 4, 5.

3. Not a neophyte—1, 2.

4. Not a drunkard (substance abuser)—1, 2, 3.

5. Not violent, quick-tempered, quarrelsome, arrogant, or overbearing—1, 2, 3, 4, 5.

6. Not a lover of money or a pursuer of dishonest gain—2, 3.

7. Gentle in his dealings with men—2, 3, 4, 5.

8. Upright and holy in his life before God—1, 2, 3, 4, 5.

9. Loves what is good—1, 2, 4, 5.

10. Faithful monogamy, with a well-ordered home and disciplined children—1, 2, 5.

11. Hospitable—2.

12. An apt teacher—2, 4.

13. Leader-developer rather than heroic leader—1, 2, 4, 5.

14. Can develop a ministry vision that respects congregational, community, and world needs—1, 2, 4, 5.

15. Can translate that vision into a concrete plan—2, 4, 5.

16. Can make and stay within a realistic budget—2, 3.

17. Can motivate others to become part of the vision through healthy means—2, 4, 5.

18. Can maintain control of a church and its programs in a healthy manner—2, 5.

19. Can build group cohesion and healthy pride—2, 5.

20. Can coach others to their best performance—2.

21. Sets an example for others to follow—2, 4, 5.

22. Earns the loyalty of staff and congregation—2.

23. Cares deeply about his congregation—1, 2, 5.

24. Is available and visible to staff and congregation—2.

You may add other specific qualities based on your self-study and your discussion of controversial issues. Then decide where you will include questions that will address these qualities. The twenty-four items noted here will be addressed either explicitly or implicitly at the data-gathering places listed if you use the questions suggested in this book. If you choose not to screen for some of these qualities, you may wish to remove the questions related to them.

Pastor's Information Form

An example of this form is included as Appendix E. Your church may make copies of this form or may use it in modified form for your pastoral search without further permission from this publisher or author. You have the same permission to use any of the other forms or form letters included at the end of this book.

Using a standard form rather than simply requesting resumes has certain advantages. First, an entire new industry has grown up that does nothing but produce resumes. These resume writers are trained to cover up failures or weaknesses in a person's work history by choosing whichever kind of resume style most easily disguises the weaknesses or failures the person may possess.

Second, professional resume writers are trained in using words that cónnote power and exceptional performance and in selecting special types of paper and typefaces that increase readability and prestige. Applicant B may look much stronger on paper than Applicant A, even though Applicant A's work history is stronger than Applicant B's, because Applicant A prepared his resume and did not know some of these techniques.

Third, resumes do not always answer the questions you would like answered. They are unlikely, for example, to include information on a previous marriage, which may be important to some churches. They usually do not volunteer information about whether the applicant has ever committed a misdemeanor or felony. They are unlikely to contain information about specific skills that you are looking for in your next pastor in light of your self-study.

Fourth, with resumes you cannot compare pastors on the same criteria; therefore, making objective comparisons between them is difficult. Incidental factors, such as whether a pastor felt it was good stewardship to pay $250 to a resume service to have a powerful-looking resume, may affect the committee more than the actual qualities of the applicant.

For those reasons, I think it is wise to compose a standard form for all applicants. Pastors who have a resume can send it along with a completed Pastor's Information Form.

Some potential applicants will not want to take the time to complete a Pastor's Information Form, particularly if they already have prepared a resume. However, a person who is unwilling to spend an hour completing an important application is probably not very motivated about coming to your church anyway. If you add several questions to the sample Pastor's Information Form, you may want to consider deleting something. An overly long form may discourage potential applicants from completing it.

Information from References

In my interviews one of the most common mistakes identified about pulpit committees was their failure to carefully check references. Most committees that do use references asked for written letters of reference. Most written letters of reference are probably little better than worthless for several reasons. Usually the people listed as references feel kindly toward the applicant. Friends don't want to cause him to be rejected for a position. They are unlikely to say anything in a letter of recommendation that would seriously jeopardize his application, even if they know of such information.

Second, in an increasingly litigious society, people are becoming reluctant to put in writing anything negative about a person, especially if they have little guarantee that this nominating committee will use what they have written confidentially. It's safer to write a letter that has vaguely positive comments than to tell an unknown committee about specific deficiencies.

Third, when receiving a letter from a reference, we lose much of the communication data that we could gain from a telephone interview. Listening to a person, we can hear the long pauses, the lack of enthusiasm in the voice tone, or the guardedness that suggests things are not what they should be. In a telephone interview we can follow up on these hesitations and often learn about information that we would never gain from a written letter. Professional search consultant Robert Dingman says, "Professionals in executive search consulting almost never use written references because of their negligible value."[36]

I strongly recommend that two or three committee members who are most comfortable making telephone interviews be assigned the task of contacting the references of applicants under serious consideration. These people should have good "telephone presence," that is, the ability to convey warmth and genuineness, trustworthiness and professionalism through their words and voice tone, for the call will often be the only means of contact with the reference.

How do we get a reference to open up and discuss less-than-positive characteristics about someone else? Robert Dingman has the following excellent advice:

> First, open the reference check with the assurance of absolute confidentiality within the search committee. You may choose to say that the reference will be shared "without attribution." That is, that the reference's name will not be disclosed, even to the search committee, but only identified as "a board member," "a deacon," "faculty member" or whatever. This assurance can help to loosen up a reluctant source.
>
> And be sure you honor your word when you promise confidentiality!
>
> Second, you can remind the source you are contacting that he is only one of a number of people you are checking with. In effect, you are saying that nothing he or she says will by itself cause the candidate to be dropped. You ease the contact's sense of guilt in this manner.
>
> Third, you can still activate a sense of prospective guilt in references by posing your questions in such a way that they would need to lie, if they did not respond honestly to your questions. While they may not want to damage the candidate's standing they normally will choose to do that rather than lie to you. Awareness of this approach can be a useful insight.
>
> Fourth, if significant negative information develops, get off that particular point as soon as you can and avoid judgmental reactions. Also, be sure to conclude the reference check on an upbeat note.[37]

A telephone reference form can be developed using the criteria the committee developed. A sample telephone interview form is included as Appendix F.

Credit and Police Records Check

This check may seem inappropriate when evaluating a pastor, but some churches have learned a lesson the hard way by not doing it. There is a biblical basis for doing this kind of check: a criterion for those who would be pastors is that their personal character be without reproach both within and without the church.

Doing such a check does not mean that an applicant would be automatically disqualified if the committee finds something. Each committee would have to make a decision about this issue based on the nature of the offense, the length of time since the offense, and evidence of repentance and personal work (perhaps through counseling) that shows the applicant has built safeguards into his life that decrease the chance of the offense recurring.

If a committee decides to do a credit and police records check, calls to the local police or to an attorney will usually furnish information on how to proceed. The applicant has given permission to do such an investigation if he has signed the release at the end of the Pastor's Information Form (see Appendix E).

Analysis of Sermons

By this time, each applicant should have sent the committee two sermons. Listening to the sermons of all the applicants will not be necessary. The committee will have eliminated many applicants in the first review (see Appendix B). For the remaining applicants, some PNC members may be assigned to make the telephone calls to their references. The rest of the members may be assigned to evaluate tapes of sermons.

See Appendix G for one method for evaluating sermons. Your committee may use it, either as it is or in modified form, or you may develop your own method for evaluating sermons. I would recommend that at least three PNC members listen to each sermon, since some committee members may have idiosyncratic preferences that do not accurately represent the preferences of the congregation. Because three people individually rate each sermon, the combined ratings will be more likely to accurately represent the congregation's preferences. For the ratings to have maximum predictive validity, each rater should evaluate the sermons without knowledge of how others have rated them. The chair of the PNC, or someone he or she designates, can be responsible for the calculations involved in quantifying and averaging those responses that can be quantified.

A Personal Interview

This fifth means of evaluating a candidate will not occur until there has been a second round of eliminations based on the committee's evaluation of sermon tapes and information gathered from interviews with references. For that reason discussion of preparation for that interview will be deferred until a later chapter.

5

*Developing a Salary
and Benefit Package*

Reasons We Should Pay Our Pastors Well

It's the Humane Thing to Do

We should be concerned about paying our pastor fairly for
several reasons. Here is one of them.

Clergy on Welfare

Picture your pastor standing in line for food stamps. It does
happen. Many clergy today find it necessary to receive
government assistance to feed their families; I am one of them.

I'm a full-time pastor of an upper-middle-class church of 300
members in a mainline denomination. I have a B.A. degree in
psychology and a master of divinity degree from a major
seminary. I've been married twelve years and have two
children. I have committed my life to Christ.

Yet the government has to supplement my income by
providing food stamps as well as the Earned Income Credit,
which comes through my income taxes, and the free lunch
program that my daughter receives in the public school.

How can this be? Even though lay people attempt to do all
they can to alleviate world suffering, they often allow their
pastors to subsist on the lowest level of income possible.

My wife and I were once able to say we earned everything

we received. We worked hard and were paid accordingly. In the ministry it's different. I work all available hours as the "pastor in charge." Whether I work forty hours or eighty hours I receive the same salary, even though I might drive twice the number of miles and spend twice as much for expenses. The harder I work, the more unreimbursed expenses I incur.

Maybe you think my wife should work outside the home. But our children are small, and with the strains of parsonage life, we believe they need their mother's presence.

Somehow it all seems wrong. The pastor should be free to serve God and the people who need him without having to fight the depressing battle of staying alive financially. The pastor's children should not have to grow up in such stark contrast to the lifestyles of the children whose church he serves. They should not have to be "second-class" citizens.

If those who are lay leaders in the churches would give thought to this social problem of the twentieth-century pastor, improvements would be made. The expenses of the ministry are higher than ever and should come out of the church's treasury. The members should sincerely try to determine what their pastor's family needs in the way of financial support. What is your pastor doing without? More important, what is his family doing without? Are his children growing up with a good impression of the church's love and care? Will they be able to receive the necessary education to cope in an increasingly technological world?

Is your pastor eligible for welfare?

—Anonymous[1]

It's the Biblical Thing to Do

Some persons justify paying pastors poorly because of the verse stating that pastors are not to be lovers of money (see 1 Tim. 3:3). To this, Fred Smith quipped, "We accuse pastors of loving money when they don't have any money to love."[2]

There is a vast chasm between the required criterion that those who wish to be pastors are not to be lovers of money and the conclusion that therefore we should not pay them an equitable and reasonable professional salary. Indeed, failure to

121

pay our pastors fairly for their work contradicts several clear passages of Scripture. Let's review them briefly.

The precedent for financially supporting our spiritual leaders began in the Pentateuch. God said, "I give to the Levites as their inheritance the tithes that the Israelites present as an offering to the LORD" (Num. 18:24 NIV).

Similarly, as Jesus sent the apostles out on their first missionary tour, He reaffirmed the principle that spiritual leaders should be supported financially by persons to whom they ministered. He said, "Do not take along any gold or silver or copper in your belts; take no bag for the journey, or extra tunic, or sandals or a staff; for the worker is worth his keep" (Matt. 10:9–10 NIV). A short time later, as Jesus sent out the seventy, He gave similar instructions (see Luke 10:1–7).

God reaffirmed this principle in the early church. The apostle Paul teaches in 1 Corinthians 9:14 that "the Lord has commanded that those who preach the gospel should receive their living from the gospel" (NIV). In 1 Timothy 5:17–18 Paul writes, "The elders who direct the affairs of the church well are worthy of double honor, especially those whose work is preaching and teaching. For the Scripture says, 'Do not muzzle the ox while it is treading out the grain,' and 'The worker deserves his wages'" (NIV).

In the verses from 1 Timothy the apostle is saying that we should be generous in the way we treat effective pastors, considering them worthy of double honor. Connecting this idea with the comment about wages indicates that the church should show this double honor through the financial support given the pastor.

Looking at the verses carefully, we see that Paul doesn't actually tell the church to pay pastors twice as much as the normal wage of that day but to consider them worthy of such. The intent is that rather than be stingy with how we pay our pastors, we should have a generous spirit in how we treat them financially.

Those verses pertain to the entire church. In Galatians 6:6 Paul speaks to us individually when he commands, "Anyone who receives instruction in the word must share all good things with his instructor" (NIV). This verse suggests that we should be generous not just in supporting our pastor with our finances but with all the good things God gives us (for example, inviting our pastor and his family to enjoy our vacation home for a week, or sharing produce from our garden, etc.). Thus, when we think of salaries for our pastoral staff, our attitude should be one of grateful generosity that God has blessed our lives by their presence and their teaching.[3]

It's the Prudent Thing to Do

We've seen that paying our pastoral staff well is both the humane thing to do and the biblical thing to do. But a third reason should motivate us, even out of selfish considerations if for no other reason. If we have an effective pastor and we aren't willing to pay him fairly for his work, we'll probably lose him to a church that will.

Pastors don't like to uproot their families, nor do they like to leave people they've come to know and love. But sometimes they realize that they must move to another church to be able to support their family above the poverty level. The present church has grown so accustomed to paying the pastor poorly, the leadership is so unwilling to recognize the drastic need for some "catching up" on staff wage levels, that there is almost no likelihood that the pastor will ever be paid a fair wage if he remains in that church. Let's all reexamine our salary structures before we lose valued pastoral staff.

How Should We Go About Setting Salaries?

Churches have developed all sorts of ways of setting salaries. Sometimes a particular individual—a banker or an accountant in the church—is designated to make a recommendation. The well-being of the pastor and his family is very much affected by the stinginess or generosity of this one individual. Since bankers and accountants are usually concerned about saving money for an organization, the scales may often tip to the stingy end of the spectrum.

In other churches, most notably congregational churches, the entire congregation may have a part in the deliberations about the pastor's salary. Manfred Holck, writing in *Leadership* magazine, says,

> There is no practical way in which an entire congregation can get involved and still come out with a plan that's reasonable, fair, and attractive to the pastor. Letting members vote in congregational meetings on the pastor's pay can be disastrous—to the congregation and to the preacher. Every member will have his or her own notion of what ought to be paid. Members with the lowest salary will believe any proposal above a bare minimum is extravagant (after all, the pastor is serving the Lord; money should not be a consideration!). Others will believe the pay is too low and demeaning for the pastor of their church. Many will believe an average member's pay will be quite all right. But all—including the preacher—may disagree on what is best.[4]

I believe it is wise for every church to have a personnel committee. This committee, along with the pastor, should develop job descriptions for each salaried position within the church. In addition, the personnel committee is responsible for finding out appropriate salaries and supplemental benefits for each staff position of the church and for making recommendations regarding them to the board each year. In this way the pastor and staff don't have to be in the awkward position of having to ask the board to consider salary and cost-of-living increases each year—a small group of people has accepted the responsibility of "looking out" for them. This group can also be authorized to investigate the best companies to provide supplemental benefits such as disability, life, and health insurance. These people should usually be professionals who are aware of salaries and benefits offered in the secular world and who have a commitment to making sure the church takes care of those who take care of it.

Holck also recommends that the discussion of specifics should occur within the personnel committee or between that committee and the board:

> Congregational action, if required, should be routine. It is simply unfair to the pastor and the pastor's family to go through severe congregational questioning concerning that which has already been thoroughly and carefully discussed by knowledgeable committee members and the board.[5]

I agree. Having sat through many congregational meetings, I think it is demeaning to our pastors for all congregational members to know every aspect of their salaries and benefits and to be able to comment on whether they think they are too high or too low. One way to offer some protection to the staff is to combine figures for all staff in the annual budget and simply provide totals. If people demand more specific information, the chair of the personnel committee can explain the general procedures the committee used in arriving at fair salary and benefit packages and say that the committee and the board have decided not to continue the practice of listing individual salaries anymore.

Factors Involved in Determining Compensation

Once the board or committee has been designated to recommend a compensation package, what factors should be considered in making a recommendation? Generally the following factors are reasonable to include:

- Education. A person who has spent four years in college and three years in seminary has seven less working years available to him than the person who has done neither. He also may have significant debt accumulated because of his training. It is reasonable to pay him a proportionally higher salary to make up for losses he incurred during training.

- Experience. Experience allows a person to be more productive for an organization, so it is reasonable to pay higher salaries to someone with more pastoral experience.
- Comparison with other professionals. There is wide diversity among professionals in various fields. We seem willing to pay outlandish salaries for some activities that have questionable benefit to our society, and so comparisons are not always a valid method. Yet there is some value in trying to find other professional careers that are similar in some way to that of pastor and compare salary and benefits in the two careers. The profession of teaching has sometimes been used since the training required for the two careers is similar in length, although the fact that pastors work twelve months rather than nine months per year should be factored into this comparison. Over the last twenty-four years the pastorate has lost considerable ground to teachers: teachers' salaries have quadrupled (as have most other salaries), while pastors' salaries have gone up only two and one-half times.[6]

Besides not having kept pace with increases in other professions over the last quarter century, pastors' salaries have not kept up with other professions in another way, discussed by Lyle Schaller. He says,

> A larger proportion of ministers' wives are working outside the home on a full-time basis than in any other profession. This includes doctors, lawyers, dentists, teachers and others. It is a must situation in many cases; the minister's wife has to supplement her husband's inadequate income.[7]

- Cost of living in a specific geographical region. Living in the Northeast and West is generally more expensive than in other parts of the country. City living is usually more expensive than suburban living, which is usually more expensive than rural living.

- Cost-of-living adjustments. If your church does not have some way of making these adjustments annually, your staff's buying power may be decreasing the longer they serve you faithfully.
- Recognition of meritorious service. Every organization should have some way of recognizing quality work and rewarding a person for the effort necessary to produce superior results.
- Leadership responsibility. Some churches build in a salary differential that considers the greater responsibility involved in caring for a congregation of 500 people than one of 120. However, size of church and workload are not always correlated. In a small church often one pastor does everything, and people may expect a higher level of personal attention. In a larger church there may be multiple staff and capable laypeople to share the work. Also, people in the larger church may not expect as much personal attention. Therefore, an argument could be made that the solo pastor in a small church deserves to be paid as much as the individual pastors of a multiple staff in a larger church.
- Reimbursable expenses. Many things a pastor does cost money, whether he is driving to the hospital several days a week to make visits, having a supportive lunch with a congregation member who has just lost his job, or following up on a host of other tasks. If the church does not have a comprehensive plan for reimbursement, the pastor is in the predicament that the more ministry he does, the less income he has to take home to his family.
- Costs involved in staying current. Every professional needs to have ways of staying current in his field. Every pastor needs to have new input so that his messages can remain vital and interesting. In other professions the employing organization ordinarily bears the costs involved in staying current. To be fair to pastors, the same should be true for them.
- Supplemental benefits. Holck says, "It is estimated that 30

to 40 percent of the typical worker's total compensation in- cludes supplemental benefits. Only 60 to 70 percent is paid in salary."[8] A national survey of pastors done in 1981 found that the average pastor's supplemental benefits were 12 percent of his base salary.[9]

- What can the church afford? With smaller churches or with churches that have a large debt load there may be a signifi- cant disparity between what the church should pay a pastor as a fair salary and what it can afford to pay him. A generally accepted criterion is that salaries should not consume more than 40 percent of a church's total income.

What should be done in such a situation? Affirm to the ap- plicant that the board knows that it cannot afford to pay him what it should but it commits to increasing the pastor's salary as a matter of priority. Sometimes church members can be encouraged to give more through sermons on tithing and on giving to the Lord beyond the tithe. An inappropriate re- sponse is to take advantage of the nonassertiveness of some young ministers and of their commitment to serving the Lord by continuing a practice of unfairly low payments for their work.

The Specifics of Determining Salary and Benefits

In the last few years an organization has become increas- ingly well known in the church administration field—the Na- tional Association of Church Business Administration. Its address is 7001 Grapevine Highway, Suite 324, Fort Worth, Texas 76180-5103, and its telephone number is (817) 284- 1732. This organization produces many helpful books and seminars related to various aspects of church administration. Of particular interest to this discussion is that it produces comprehensive salary surveys of various church staff posi- tions and breaks them down statistically by region of the country and denomination. These figures, then, can be a helpful starting point in salary determinations.*

However, data on what other churches are paying their pastors should be only part of a church's approach in determining what to offer a pastor. If churches as a group are underpaying their pastors for their work, simply taking a figure from the NACBA's book and using it continues the process of underpayment.

I would recommend that another method be used along with the figures from NACBA to estimate how much a pastor should be paid based on the salaries of his church members. Harold Sedrel, a management consultant for many years who has written several pamphlets regarding clergy compensation, developed the basic steps in this method.[10] The method can be broken into eight steps.

1. Obtain the median family income estimates for the area where the church is located.

Many writers and consultants agree that the median family income is a good base from which to start. If the pastor's salary is lower than the typical family income of his congregation, he is likely to feel financially mistreated by them. But a pastor's income significantly higher than that of the typical family may adversely affect congregational morale and giving.

Theoretically it should be possible to anonymously poll a congregation and from that develop a median family income. However, this approach is often hampered by logistical problems. Probably an easier way is to identify the county or counties from which the church draws its congregation. Then by going to the current issue of *Sales and Marketing Management Magazine*'s "Survey of Buying Power," extract the Median Household Effective Buying Income (MHEBI) for that county or counties. (This magazine is often available in libraries or Chamber of Commerce offices.) Multiply this num-

---

*The *1990–1991 National Church Staff Compensation Survey* is available from NACBA for $49.00. A second book, *Salary Administration,* provides a model for developing salary structures and is available from NACBA for $8.00.

ber by 1.*xx*, where *xx* equals the inflation rate for the past year. That will give you an estimate of the MHEBI for your locality for the coming year.

For example, if the MHEBI for your county was $32,000.00 and the inflation index for the past twelve months has been 7 percent, the estimated MHEBI for the coming year would be

$$\$32,000.00 \times 1.07 = \$34,240.00$$

If your church draws equally from two counties, find the average MHEBI for the two, then multiply that number by 1 plus the inflation rate.[11]

2. Multiply this number by a factor that represents the education of the pastor relative to the education of the typical head of household in the congregation.

For example, if the pastor has a Master of Divinity degree (seven years of college and seminary) and the typical head of household in the congregation lacks college, preparation for ministry has shortened the pastor's working years by seven. Multiplying the median family income by 118 percent compensates him for the seven years of non-income-producing years. Instead of having forty-seven full-earning years, this pastor has forty. (Forty-seven years × 100 percent is equal to forty years × 118 percent.)

If the pastor has seven years of college and seminary and the average head of household has four years, the multiplier should be 108 percent. (Forty-three years × 100 percent is equal to forty years × 108 percent.) If the pastor attended a four-year Bible college instead of seminary, and if the average head of household also has a four-year degree, the multiplier would obviously be 1.

3. Add to this figure a factor that adjusts for the experience of your pastor.

For example, if the average teacher in your school system gets $300.00 more for each year of experience, it would be reasonable to add $300.00 for each year of pastoral experience your pastor has had since leaving seminary.

4. Adjust this amount by the size of your congregation.

The amount of pastoral, counseling, teaching and administrative responsibilities increases with the size of the church. Harold Sedrel offers the following suggestions:

Where there are approximately:	Add:
400 to 650 members	3 percent
650 to 1,000 members	6 percent
1,000 to 1,500 members	9 percent
Over 1,500 members	12 percent

5. Adjust if the church provides a parsonage.

Normally a family should not spend more than 25 percent of its income on housing. If the fair market rental value of the manse is greater than 25 percent of the pastor's salary, it is fair to subtract 25 percent from his salary in exchange for housing. If the fair market value of the manse is greater than 25 percent of the pastor's salary, it is unfair to reduce his salary by more than 25 percent. If the fair market value for renting the manse is less than 25 percent of his salary, his salary should not be reduced by an amount greater than the fair market value rental price.

This calculated figure pays for the parsonage but not for the utilities connected with it. If the parsonage is insulated poorly and has excessively high utility bills, the church may wish to provide a partial utility differential to cover the added cost above the normal cost of utilities for a house of that size in that area.

If the congregation expect the pastor and his family to use the parsonage, they in a sense have "captive tenants." They should not abuse the pastor and his family by failing to keep the parsonage in as good condition as they would if they were having to compete on the open market for tenants.

An increasing number of churches do not have parsonages, particularly in urban and suburban areas. Some pastors prefer to purchase a home rather than live in a church-owned parsonage. The benefits of this arrangement for pastors changes with the inflation rate, how often they move, the interest rate, and the state of the housing market. Probably the best solution is to have a parsonage available for pastors who prefer it; the parsonage can be used as rental property when the current pastor would prefer to purchase his own home.

6. Recognition for "ruling well."

Mr. Sedrel mentions that the board may wish to add an additional .5 percent, 1 percent, or 1.5 percent to the pastor's salary as recognition for excellent performance.

7. Add an appropriate level of supplemental benefits.

The personnel committee may wish to do some research in the local community to find an average for supplemental benefits of other professional workers. This amount usually is between 30 and 40 percent of one's cash salary. It can be spent on medical, dental, disability, professional liability insurance, retirement fund, and so on. Since some pastors have chosen to be classified as self-employed (and therefore the church does not have to pay the income tax), some churches have decided to help him pay his social security self-employment tax.

8. Items that should be budgeted for but should not be considered salary.

These items include reimbursement for miles driven when engaged in church work, reimbursement for discretionary, benevolence, and hospitality funds used in his church work. Every pastor needs means for having new material so that he does not become stagnant. Unanimously, church consultants recommend that he be given a continuing education fund that he can use to purchase books and periodicals or attend seminars and workshops. If the pastor and his wife are expected to attend state or national denominational meetings, their costs for these meetings should be covered.

How Many Hours Should Pastors Work?

In return for a fair salary, how many hours should a pastor be expected to work? We have all known pastors who worked incredible numbers of hours each week, and sometimes we hold an unconscious belief that a truly committed pastor will follow their example. Yet often the results of such unstinting service are broken families and broken marriages. Surely that is not God's will for a pastor (see 1 Tim. 3:4–5; Titus 1:6). On the other hand more things always need to be done in a church, sometimes very pressing and important things. There are always sick or hospitalized persons who could benefit from a pastoral visit. There is always more that could be done to refine a sermon. There are always committee members who would be encouraged if the pastor attended their meetings. What expectations should a pastor have of himself and should his board have of him?

Harold Sedrel has written a paper called "The Pastor's Time" in which he develops the following ideas.[12] The average professional works between forty and fifty hours per week at his profession. An average of forty-five hours per week is probably a reasonable estimate. In addition, many committed Christians also donate an average of four to six hours per week to work for the Lord, whether they are preparing for and teaching Sunday school, singing in the choir, or involved in some other ministry. How the person spends these hours is up to him—finding one or more activities that are compatible with his skills and are personally fulfilling for him.

Sedrel suggests that asking for the same kind of commitment from a pastor is fair—roughly forty-five hours per week in normal pastoral activities, with the possibility of another four to six hours spent doing things in the Lord's work at which he is skilled and which he finds personally fulfilling. Widely respected Alban consultant Roy Oswald also recommends an average of fifty hours per week.[13] If we work more than fifty hours per week for an extended period of time, our lives are likely to become unbalanced in one or more areas. We will not have the time to devote to our spouses and our children that they need in order to feel loved and cared for.

Some Closing Comments

If in working through these steps, members of the PNC realize that the salaries the church has offered in the past are significantly below a fair wage scale, this can be an opportune time to have a meeting with either the board or the finance committee to go over the material in this chapter and initiate a review.

Normally the PNC does not have the authority to make changes in salaries, but it can initiate a discussion with those who have the authority to make such changes. If church salaries are significantly below what they should be, finding a new pastor who will come to the church may be difficult, and the pastor will be more likely to leave in a few years for a church that will pay him more fairly.

6

Finding and Contacting Pastoral Applicants

The process of finding and initially contacting pastoral applicants can be divided into seven sequential steps. This chapter describes those steps.

One, based on the primary needs identified in the self-study, outline the qualifications of the new pastor.[1] The job description is not as important as the job qualifications since the job description of senior pastor is similar in most denominations.* The job description is important only if it deviates in some way(s) from the standard one.

Similarly, it is not necessary to explain job qualifications that every denomination routinely accepts. What is more important is identifying those qualifications that may be specific to your church. Specific qualifications might include "can converse in both English and Spanish" or "can serve as a mediator and peacemaker between groups within the church that have a long history of conflict."

Two, after the necessary skills have been identified, ask, Who

---

*Here is a typical job description for a senior pastor: "Responsible for all activities of the church. Responsibilities regularly include conducting services, making visitations, performing special ceremonies such as weddings or funerals, counseling, leading business meetings and overseeing the work of other church staff members" (taken from *Christian Ministries Salary Survey,* 7th ed., p. 98).

might have this set of skills? The five most obvious kinds of people would be

- pastors who are already employed in full-time church work,
- those with pastoral training who are not presently in full-time church work,
- missionaries who can no longer remain on the mission field because of health, family, or other reasons,
- teachers in Bible colleges or seminaries who might be interested in returning to the pastorate, and
- those working in denominational administration who might be interested in returning to the pastorate.

Through brainstorming, your committee may be able to identify other possible areas to search.

Three, identify sources who would know of candidates from these areas. Begin an extensive search using telephone and mail to identify specific people for your committee to consider. At this point distinguish between *sources* and *applicants*. Sources are people who can identify one or more possible applicants for your consideration.

Before mounting an external campaign, decide whether any of your present church staff fits your pastor profile well. There are several advantages to using a present staff member if he is truly what your church needs. The church saves the expense and time involved in an external search. The person already knows the church well and has contacts in place. Some disadvantages include the possibility that a present staff member may not have a new vision for where the church could go in the next five to ten years, and he may encounter resistance if he tries to supervise former peers. The committee that seriously wants to consider a present staff member should probably not let that staff member know he is under consideration until the PNC is ready to recommend him to the congregation. Otherwise the experience of being considered and rejected may make it too painful for the staff member to remain in his present position. The PNC should probably not recommend a present staff member unless the committee believes that the congregation will strongly support the nomination. If a substantial minority will not support it, the church is likely to lose members and financial support if the congregation elects him.

Other sources of names of potential applicants include the following:

- state superintendents or overseers (these people may be good sources of names and of other ways to identify potential applicants)
- state superintendents in other states
- national denominational headquarters (some, such as the Presbyterian Church [U.S.A.] and the Episcopal Church, have a national computerized databank of pastors; other denominations probably will have this service available in coming years; for those that do not, one or more denominational departments are likely to be able to supply names)
- seminaries and Bible college placement offices
- notices in denominational and interdenominational magazines
- interdenominational pastoral placement services
- congregation members (more about this to follow)
- evangelists (or other traveling speakers within your denomination who meet pastors frequently)
- individual faculty members at Bible colleges or seminaries

Management consultant, Thomas Gilmore states, "Executive recruiting firms suggest that 150 to 200 hours of telephone networking may be required to build an adequate pool of high-quality finalists for a key executive role."[2] Since pastor search committees can use a variety of methods besides telephone networking, they probably will not need to spend as much time as Gilmore suggests. However, plan to spend a significant amount of time on the telephone contacting sources and then following up on referrals.

When the committee solicits referrals from the congregation, two things are important. First, the committee should encourage the congregation to recommend names of potential applicants so that the congregation feels involved. Second, the committee should develop a system by which the recommender withdraws the recommendation if the person fails to meet the selection criteria.

One way to accomplish both objectives is to compose a recommendation sheet that lists the recommender, the recommendee, a way of contacting the recommendee, the required scriptural qualities as interpreted by the committee, the psychological qualities chosen by the committee, and any specific qualities resulting from the church's self-study. The recommender should rate the recommendee on each quality from one to five (with five being excellent, three being average, and one being significantly deficient). This procedure should prompt the recommender to withdraw the recommendation if it becomes clear that the recommendee does not meet several of the committee's required characteristics.

Four, remind committee members of the significance of confidentiality. This probably will be the first time the committee begins to identify specific individuals, and the discussions of confidentiality that occurred several weeks earlier may have faded in members' memories. Remind them that no one is to share the name or status of any applicant until and unless the committee recommends that person to the congregation as a candidate. Also remind them that they may promise referral sources confidentiality in the event that they ask a source to reveal any information that might decrease an applicant's consideration by the committee (their comments will be discussed "without attribution").

At this time arranging for confidentiality in several other areas is appropriate. Files of applicants should be stored in a place that will not be available to noncommittee members. Whoever types correspondence and does other secretarial work for the committee should agree to keep all committee work confidential. Each committee member who will be making telephone calls should plan what to say if an applicant's secretary asks the purpose of the call—otherwise the committee member may unwittingly betray the confidentiality of that applicant. For the same reason, committee members who visit a candidate's church should plan beforehand what they will say if someone asks the purpose of their visit. Committee members should be reminded that they are not to share the identities of applicants even with a spouse.[3]

Five, encourage committee members to brainstorm for names of referral sources. (As mentioned earlier, a *source* is a person who may be able to suggest candidates for the position.) Compare notes to avoid duplication. Discuss how to summarize the church and what you are looking for in a few sentences. Gilmore asserts,

> Whether the recruiter is calling a potential candidate who is already happily and productively employed or an eminent source who is extremely busy, there is a limited opportunity to get that person's attention via what Isaacson has termed "the pitch." Because selling the opportunity is so critical, the recruiter and team should, before going to the market, spend time developing, refining, and actively practicing the pitch.[4]

It is appropriate to develop a common "pitch," write it out, and have committee members practice it a few times with one another before going home and calling the sources they know. A typical conversation might include the following:

A. Introduction, purpose of call, and request for five to ten minutes of source's time.

B. Source consents to give time.

C. Describe location and size of church. Describe skills that you are looking for in a candidate that may be specific to your situation.

D. Try to obtain at least two or three names from source. After no more names are forthcoming, ask for telephone numbers or addresses of the people he or she has identified.

E. If your committee has some requirements that the source may not be aware of because they are not universally accepted (e.g., no previous marriages), ask if those requirements would disqualify any of the recommendees.

F. Confirm accuracy of names, telephone numbers or addresses, thank source for the time, and end call.

G. Make certain that all information is legible. Your sheet should include the following: (1) name of recommender, (2) name of recommendee, and (3) a way of contacting recommendee.

Six, designate one or two persons to call all recommendees to see if they would be willing to receive information about the church and its present opening. Assure them that receiving the information implies no commitment on their part to apply. Ask the applicants if they prefer mail to be sent to the home address or to the church marked "Personal."

These designated persons should start a notebook that contains a telephone log on each person contacted. The first two pages should list all persons contacted and the page number their log appears on (since it will not be possible to enter them in alphabetical order). Each recommendee should have a page that includes the recommender, the recommendee's name, telephone number, and preferred mailing address. Each call to that recommendee should be entered in the log, with a brief discussion of the conversation and the result. This method enables the committee chairperson to know exactly what the committee has said to each recommendee and reduces chances for accidentally calling the same recommendee twice.

Seven, send a personalized cover letter on church stationery from the committee chairperson along with a small packet of information to all recommendees who agree to receive material. The packet should contain a summary of the church's self-study, including a brief history of the church, and the pastoral position that is open with a job description if the description might be ambiguous otherwise. The job description should include qualifications that may be specific to your church. The packet also should include a description of the church's current ministries, average attendance figures for the last three years, a summary of the current budget, a copy or summary of the church constitution, bylaws, and doctrinal statement. A promotional brochure describing the city and community (such as that prepared by the Chamber of Commerce) can be included along with the Pastor's Information Form. Note on the telephone log the date the committee sends each packet.

This packet should be eight pages or less. Many pastors, especially those who are relatively happy in their present setting, will not be willing to read a book of information about your church. So develop an accurate summary of the important information about your church, and present it in a way that will attract the interest of a potential applicant. The full self-study and a more in-depth discussion of problems (challenges) your church is facing will be sent to candidates you designate as "finalists."

Describing the Congregation
and Community to Candidates

William Harbin tells the following true story:

A committee visited a church to hear a prospect preach. In an interview with the pastor following the worship the committee members asked him several questions and then gave him a chance, "Now, do you have some questions you would like to ask us about our church?" The pastor replied, "Yes, how many do you average in Sunday School?" The chairman turned to a member and inquired, "John, how many do we run in Sunday School?" John said, "I meant to check that out before we left." Then the pastor said, "How much does your church give to mission causes?" The chairman turned to another member and asked, "Jane, do you remember that figure?" She replied, "Well, I did know, but I just can't remember the figure now." After the pastor received two or three other iffy replies he said, "You know, I have the name of a pastor I would like to recommend to you."[1]

If your committee does not prepare so that it can provide thorough information about your church to a candidate, you are likely to lose him as this church did. You will need to give two levels of information to applicants/candidates. Initially you will be giving them a summary of information about your church in the initial packet sent to all applicants. This summary should not be too long or else the size of the packet will discourage many potential applicants from reading it and applying for the position.

Later in the process you will have narrowed your applicants down to five or six top candidates. These pastors will want more extensive information as they make a decision about accepting or not accepting a position with your church. This chapter will discuss questions you should be prepared to answer from these candidates.

Ways of Presenting Information to Candidates

You can present this information to candidates in at least three ways. First, you can be prepared to answer questions if the candidate asks them. You give only the information the candidate requests. Probably most PNCs operate this way. Second, you can present this information to the candidate during your interview with him (whether or not he specifically asks these questions). Third, you can write out and mail this information to the candidate before the interview. There are, I believe, advantages to using this third approach.

With the first approach, the candidate is unlikely to ask enough questions so that he develops a comprehensive understanding of your church. Even if he is an exception and asks the committee questions for an hour or two, the anxiety of the interview is likely to cause him to forget portions of what your committee tells him.

In the second method, where the committee presents this information during the interview, the same problem can emerge—the candidate's anxiety may cause him to forget many of the details. Or his attention is likely to be focused on making a good impression on the committee, and he may be distracted from paying much attention to your presentation.

Mailing the material to the candidate before the interview allows him to read it more than once. Thus he can frame questions to the PNC based on an in-depth understanding of your church. Pastors who have candidated at various churches speak positively of those churches that sent a comprehensive report of the church to them before the candidating interview.

In this more in-depth presentation you should include enough of the positive features of the church and community that you motivate candidates to want to come to you. Unlike their secular counterparts, pastors are usually motivated by the opportunity to use their gifts and training in a greater ministry. Although considerations like salary and benefits are important, most pastors are primarily concerned that the church's compensation package meet the family's basic needs. Beyond that, too great an emphasis on financial and other benefits may turn off a candidate who is motivated primarily by spiritual considerations.

The wife and children are likely to be motivated by other things. Wives tend to be more concerned about the opportunity for a good education and adequate medical care in the community. They also will be interested in having a safe environment with opportunities for their children to develop friendships with other healthy children. Children, unless they are very unhappy with their present peer situation, probably will be reluctant to leave an area that represents security to them. You are most likely to motivate them to be willing to consider a change by encouraging them with the knowledge that they can develop friends quickly and by telling them about recreational opportunities for children available in your community.

To do the best job of "wooing" a candidate, you should include things in this more extensive information packet aimed at attracting the potential pastor, his spouse, and his children. After all, a move is expensive, anxiety-producing, and risky. You have to convince this family that your church and community have enough to offer them that it is worth the expense, anxiety, and risk.

Two Nontraditional Ways

Besides the typical ways of introducing a church to a candidate (either verbally or in writing), two nontraditional ways can be used in place of, or in addition to, them. Robert Dingman describes one of these ways:

> Find someone in your congregation who has a videotape camera and can use it reasonably well. Or, hire a professional. Have him do a tape covering your physical facilities. Add to that a few minutes on the tape with key church leaders and have them share their hopes for the church. You may want to add a few people, such as a spokesman for the youth group, who may not be an elected leader. I predict that such an introduction will do well in presenting your case, if your people can be fairly natural on camera.
>
> If it is possible, also put on your tape some footage that allows the candidate to get a sample of your music program. Interviews with others on the pastoral staff could also be used, if you feel it would also be a selling point. The reproducing of this tape is not expensive and is simple to do.[2]

Another nontraditional method is to have the candidate and his family visit the church anonymously for a Sunday. They can experience the congregation as the congregation normally behaves and assess whether they would feel comfortable with the group. Those pastors who have tried this approach recommend it very highly.

Your description of the church to the pastoral candidates can be either verbal or written. Because of the amount of information to present and the candidate's ability to read the information more than once, I recommend the written format. Whichever way your committee chooses to go, the information can be divided into four main categories—the history of the church; the present ministry of the church; the future plans, goals, and challenges of the church; and the expectations, role, and compensation of the pastor.[3] Much of the content in this description can come from your self-study. Some denominations emphasize certain kinds of information much more than others. Tailor the data suggested here to meet the perceived priorities within your denomination.

History of the Church

This history can include the date the church was established and if this is reasonable to do, a discussion of the pastors who have served, their dates of ministry, and some of their significant contributions. If your church has a long history, focus only on the most significant pastors of the distant past and then include a description of the last two or three recent pastors.

Most candidates will want to know the reasons pastors have ended their ministries at the church. Does the church have a history of firing pastors? How long have most pastors stayed at the church? Most candidates will particularly want to know the tenure of the last pastor, how he got along with present staff, why he left, and what he is doing now.

Present Ministry of the Church

This section will be the longest and should include the following items:

- The physical facilities of the church, including buildings, parking areas, property limitations and possibilities for future expansion, and a description of the parsonage.
- The organizational structure of the church, including the board and all important committees.
- The present salaried staff, including names, brief job descriptions, and whether they are full-time or part-time.
- The various ministries of the church, including worship services, Sunday school, Wednesday evening services, choir, orchestra, visitation, missions, children and youth programs, singles programs, programs for senior adults, prayer ministries, and so on. Many candidates will be interested in how average attendance or involvement figures for this year compare with figures from five years ago.
- Descriptions of the congregation by age, occupation, education, and ethnic groups.

- Interest of the congregation in evangelism, social concern, and involvement in the political process.
- The congregation's attitude toward giving, percentage who tithe, indebtedness of church, and manageability of present budget. How does present giving compare with five years ago?
- Church giving for other denominational ministries.
- Willingness of congregation to volunteer for leadership and service in the various church ministries.
- Operation of Christian school or day-care center, if the church has one.
- Radio or television ministry.

Future Ministry of the Church

This section can include the future ministry goals developed because of your self-study, the building program anticipated in the next two or three years, and problems needing to be resolved. Problems can sometimes legitimately be reframed as diversities within the congregation (e.g., some in the congregation are strong dispensationalists, and some are strong covenantalists) or as challenges. Challenges can include internal ones (problems coming from within the congregation) and external ones (challenges coming from the community or the world). Discuss difficulties of the church that you hope the future pastor will help you resolve. Also discuss plans for additional staff. This section can indicate businesses moving in or out of the community, urban renewal projects, or any other special problems or opportunities facing the community.

Expectations, Role, and Compensation of Pastor[4]

Your discussion here may address many of the following questions.

The Pastor in the Pulpit

- Does the congregation expect a particular style of preaching, or is the pastor free to use a variety of styles?
- What kind of study schedule do you permit your pastor to keep? For example, would the church understand the pastor's having a study in his home and reserving either the mornings or the afternoons for sermon preparation and personal study?
- What is the length of sermons you are used to?
- Is there a specific expectation about the content of Sunday morning, Sunday evening, and Wednesday evening services?
- Is the pastor expected to lead worship and deliver the sermon?
- What kinds of activities is the church accustomed to during the worship part of the service?
- Does the congregation want something different in its worship and sermons than it has presently been receiving?
- What is the congregation's attitude toward the expression of the gifts of the Spirit (charismatic gifts)?
- How often are guest speakers used?
- How often are revivals scheduled?
- What is the philosophy regarding missionary guest speakers?
- How often does the church observe ordinances of Communion and baptism?
- What is the church's philosophy regarding baby dedications?
- Are there special traditions connected with homecoming, Christmas, the new year, and Easter?
- What are the church's expectations regarding weddings, who can be married in the church, and funerals?

The Pastor and His Staff

- Does the church have a history of team cooperation?
- What is the size of the church staff?

- Does the pastor have a personal secretary?
- At what point would the church consider adding additional staff members?
- What are the general compensation and benefits for staff members?
- Who does the staff answer to—the board, elders, or senior pastor?
- What is the method of hiring and firing staff members?
- Were staff members asked to stay in their positions? If so, what have they been promised in terms of continuance?
- Is there a personnel committee (by that or another name) with the responsibility of revising salaries and benefits to keep them similar to those of the general community? Have personnel policies been developed? If so, include them.
- Is there a flow chart describing the basic structure of the church organization? Is the church organization presbyterial, episcopal, congregational, or some mixture?

The Pastor's Role in Building and Maintenance

- Who is responsible for maintaining the church and parsonage in good repair? What is the process used to approve and finance such repairs?
- Does the church have a master plan for future buildings? Are there needs for immediate building in the next year or two? What role is the pastor expected to play in oversight of new buildings?

The Pastor's Priorities

- What are the congregation's expectations regarding the emphasis and time the pastor allocates to each of the following: sermon preparation, teaching, church administration, counseling, hospital and home visitation, building coordination, denominational involvement at the district, state, and national levels?
- Who does most of the counseling?

- How would the congregation respond if a pastor acknowledged that he did not believe counseling was one of his gifts and referred such requests to other staff or to outside counselors?
- How does the congregation feel about the pastor's involvement with denominational affairs at the district, state, and national levels? Does the church pay expenses when the pastor attends such meetings?
- How does the congregation feel about the pastor speaking at other churches or conducting revivals or mission trips?

The Pastor's Personal Life

- What is the church's philosophy concerning the pastor's time off with his family?
- What is the church's expectation regarding a normal work week for the pastor? Days off?
- What is the church members' practice regarding calling the pastor at home for nonemergency reasons?
- What is the church's expectation regarding the pastor's wife's involvement in church activities?

The Pastor's Compensation

- What is the general salary range being offered for this position?
- What factors are considered in setting salaries?
- What other benefits besides basic salary are offered?
- How often are cost-of-living, salary, and benefits adjustments made? Is this process automatic, or does it have to be initiated by the pastor?
- What is the process used to reimburse the pastor for mileage and other costs associated with pastoral ministry?
- What funds are designated to help the pastor keep current and fresh in his preaching and church growth ideas?
- Does the church participate in retirement and social security?

- What vacation times are given to the pastor?
- Are funds designated for moving expenses of a new pastor?
- Is there a parsonage? Is the pastor expected to live in it, or does he have a choice?
- If the pastorate is a part-time position, what time is allowed for school or secular work?

Miscellaneous

- What attitude does the church take toward divorced and re-married people (also include any other group about which there is some controversy in your denomination)?
- What is the general attitude toward social drinking or drinking in moderation?
- What is the attitude toward smoking or the use of tobacco?
- What is the church's attitude toward church discipline? Does the church have a written policy regarding it?
- What is the general attitude about the longevity of the pastorate? Does the church expect a pastor to make a commitment for a specific length of time?
- Where are you now in your process of selecting a pastor?
- What process do you intend to use to make a final decision (i.e., will you present several candidates to the congregation, or your highest candidate, let them make a decision, next candidate, etc.?)?

Conclusion

As you can see, the amount of material presented here would make it difficult to tell all this in an interview, and for that reason I recommend writing it out, asking candidates to keep the material regarding church problems confidential, and sending it to your top five or six candidates. Then the candidate and his wife can carefully read the material and come to the interview with any follow-up questions. And you can use most of the time in the interview asking the candidate questions since you will already have answered many of his.

Screening and Selecting Pastoral Candidates

Presenting Candidates to the Congregation

A Brief Recapitulation

To review briefly where we are in the selection process you can turn to Appendix B (Chart for Guiding the Board and PNC During the Transition Process). You have sent out the initial information packet and Pastor's Information Form to applicants and potential applicants whom you have identified by talking with your referral sources (Step 18). Within two months you may have between twenty and fifty completed applications. Your task now is to reduce the applicant pool by a first round of eliminations.

Do not allow any of these applicants to be a guest speaker until you have completed the screening process. Leonard Hill tells of a congregational church where a man who was an applicant offered to preach for a Sunday. During the service, which went well, he let the congregation know that he was a candidate for their pastoral vacancy. The congregation moved to vote on his candidacy immediately and chose the man as their next pastor before the nominating committee had any information about his conversion, experience, or anything else![1]

The First "Cut"

At this point you should have the completed Pastor's Information Forms (PIFs) and academic transcripts from your applicants. Your first round of eliminations separates those who clearly do not meet your pastor profile from those who more closely approximate it. Applicants can be divided into three categories during this cut—those who are clearly unacceptable, those who are unlikely, and those who possibly meet your criteria.[2]

The decision about who should be in which category depends on data easily found in the applicants' PIFs and transcripts. Here are some questions to ask:[3]

1. Does this applicant have the educational background that prepares him for ministry and that also will prepare him to work comfortably with your congregation? (This question is particularly relevant if your congregation is well educated.)

2. How did this applicant use his educational years? Do his transcripts reflect someone who was a good steward of those experiences?

3. How much experience has he had in the pastorate?

4. Has he had opportunities to develop the specific skills he would need in your church?

5. Is his age compatible with what you need?

6. What has been the average tenure of his churches (i.e., does he show a stable or unstable work history?)?

If you have many applicants in your "Possibles" category, you may choose to send nonacceptance letters to applicants in your "Unacceptable" and "Unlikely" categories. If you have only a few applicants in your "Possibles" category, you may wish to send nonacceptance letters only to those in your "Unacceptable" category, and not make a decision regarding those in your "Unlikely" category at this time. Appendix H includes several letters you may use in this process.

The Second "Cut"

The second round of eliminations requires finer discrimination and more committee time than the first one. Assign one or more persons to conduct the telephone reference interviews and divide the "Possible" candidates between them. Try to get feedback from other people who know the applicant to add to information from the references he listed.

References can be obtained from members of previous churches where he has served (but not a church where he is currently serving), staff members of churches where he has previously worked, other pastors, others in the church's community, district and state denominational staff, and college and seminary faculty.[4] Appendix F can be a guide when you do reference checks. (Remember to honor any promises of anonymity by including the person's input without revealing the identity.) An increasing number of PNCs also do a credit check and a police records check.

The remainder of the committee can listen to sermon tapes and evaluate them. Appendix G is a sermon evaluation sheet. You can use it as is or modify it based on the criteria most relevant for your congregation. The rating you give will help you compare the strengths of applicants. Listening to tapes also gives an abundance of clues whether there would be a good fit between your congregation and the applicant. Listen to his vocabulary to determine whether it suggests an educational level compatible with your congregation (a highly educated pastor with a working-class congregation may be just as much a misfit as someone who murders the King's English in a well-educated congregation).

Consider how well the applicant can express the struggles of one's inner spiritual life. Some congregations tend to deal with inner struggles by repressing their awareness of the struggles; for them, a pastor who was vulnerable and transparent probably would be too threatening. Other congregations want a pastor who can articulate the inner struggles that we as Christians experience; they will be unhappy with a pastor who represses such struggles.

Pay attention to how "right-brained" versus "left-brained" an applicant may be in comparison to your congregation. Although this is somewhat of an oversimplification, people who are right-brain dominant tend to be intuitive and more experientially oriented. People who are left-brain dominant tend to be more cognitive and rational and often are not intuitive or experientially oriented. Obviously, pastors who are extreme in either direction will have more difficulty satisfying their congregations than pastors who are closer to the middle. However, if a congregation is composed of people who like either of these extremes, a pastor who is like them will be well accepted.

Based on your committee's evaluation of the references and sermons, do your second round of eliminating, narrowing your "Possible" candidates down to the top five or six. After you have selected your finalists, check with each one by telephone and do the following:

A. Let him know that he is one of five or six finalists.

B. Confirm whether he still wishes to be considered for the position.

C. If he is, tell him that you will send a more in-depth packet of information about the church that he and his spouse may read.

D. Ask them to keep the information regarding problems in the church confidential.

E. Schedule a three-hour interview with each finalist.

It may not be necessary to use the entire three hours, but it is better to have extra time than to have inadequate time. I would recommend that you not conduct more than two interviews per week. Otherwise your committee members will become overtired, and they will begin to confuse one applicant with another. One interview per week is probably optimal, although your committee may want to speed up the process by having more than one.

You should offer to pay the applicant and his spouse's travel expenses. Sometimes applicants live so far away that paying their expenses for this trip is prohibitive. One alternative is to have a conference call, using a group speakerphone for your committee, and having the applicant and his wife on extensions or on a speakerphone at their end. A disadvantage of this arrangement is that you cannot assess the applicant's nonverbal behavior and his "presence." However, if there were something significantly deficient or exceptional about this, the telephone reference calls should have picked it up. In this situation you might also ask him to send a videotape of him delivering a sermon.

Interviewing the Finalists

Some persons question the validity of the executive interview. Thomas Gilmore summarizes some criticisms:

> Interviewing is a frequent method of assessment in executive selection, yet the empirical research (mostly conducted on lower-level jobs) is not encouraging about interviews' effectiveness for accurate screening (Arvey and Campion, 1982). Interviewers often disagree significantly in their appraisals of candidates. First impressions often dominate; interviewers sometimes reach their initial decisions in the first quarter of the interview. Unfavorable impressions can be created quickly from very few negative items, yet favorable impressions build slowly. Recall of information from interviews is often extremely poor. Many interviewers compare the candidates to two clusters of attributes that they use across vast ranges of different jobs: personal-relations attributes, and attributes of the good corporate citizen—trustworthy, dependable, conscientious, and so on (Morgan, n.d.).
>
> In the executive search, interviews add another source of information to the image of a candidate, although most

seasoned recruiters place more stock in past performance than in the interview.[5]

Another concern is that typical group interviewers often fail to prepare and coordinate their questions with one another beforehand, which can result in awkward silences. Each interviewer may pursue questions that he or she thinks up. Frequently, another interviewer inserts a second line of questions before the applicant has an opportunity to talk about the first issue in depth. As a result, the applicant often experiences such interviews as disorganized. The PNC does not have an opportunity to understand the applicant's views in depth on many issues.

To address some of these difficulties, the PNC can do the following:

1. Give greater weight to the applicant's demonstrated abilities than to his ability to engage them interpersonally in the interview.

2. Be aware of the tendency to make premature decisions based on the first few minutes of the interview. Consciously try to suspend making a decision about the applicant until its end.

3. Constantly compare the applicant to the criteria developed in the self-study rather than to the general interpersonal skills and good "corporate citizenship."

4. Develop an organized plan for how the group will ask questions so that they discuss all essential topics in depth.

One possible plan is to list beforehand questions that an applicant will be asked and the order in which they will be asked. Then let each committee member volunteer to ask certain ones. (You will probably ask all applicants a common core of questions and then a few specific ones for each individual based on information in the PIF, telephone references, and sermons.)

Each person who volunteers for a question is responsible

for asking that question and any follow-up question(s) necessary to clarify the applicant's answer. Anyone else may ask a follow-up question on that topic as well. The committee chair can check to see if there are any further questions on that topic and then go to the next designated person and question. In this way committee members ask all questions on a given topic at once, giving the feeling of a more organized discussion.

The questions should be organized so that the early ones touch upon topics emphasizing the applicant's strengths and successes. After the applicant and the group have built rapport and feel more comfortable with each other, the discussion can move into areas that may be more troubling for the applicant, such as difficulties he has experienced. Be sensitive to the applicant and his spouse: it's not easy to talk about personal failures with a group of unknown people, particularly when one does not know how they will respond to someone's honesty and vulnerability. Deal with each applicant with the same kind of gentleness you would want to be dealt with if you were the interviewee.

Before each interview, everyone on the nominating committee should review the applicant's answers on the PIF. Here is a possible set of questions to use or adapt if you wish to do so.[6] In some of these groups the questioner should ask one question, allow the pastor to answer it, and then ask the second question in the group. In other groups the second question clarifies the first, so both should be used together.

1. Please tell us about the home in which you grew up. What are some memories of your parents and peers that significantly shaped your attitudes toward God, toward work, and toward the values you presently hold?

2. When did you first feel God's call on your life? How did you decide to enter the ministry?

3. Can you identify the ministers, teachers, and authors who have significantly influenced your beliefs and behaviors about the ministry? What impact has each of them had on your thinking or methods of ministry?

4. Would you describe the various ministries you have had until the present? For each, please describe one or more occurrences that you believe were real successes. For each, tell at least one thing you learned about ministry by making a mistake.

5. How would you describe your style of leadership?

6. What do you believe is the healthiest relationship between a pastor, his board, the congregation, and the denomination?

7. How have your faith and your theological views changed since you entered college and seminary? Since you entered the ministry?

8. Would you describe the process you go through when you are preparing a sermon? What goals do you try to accomplish through your preaching?

9. What emphasis do you place on pastoral counseling? Please describe your training and experience in this area.

10. What is your philosophy regarding hospital and home pastoral visits?

11. What approaches to a congregation's financial stewardship do you prefer? What methods do you use to appeal to people regarding giving?

12. What in the ministry do you consider to be your specialty?

13. How much do you like to be involved in denominational activity at the district, state, and national levels?

14. What issues do you see as the most important ones facing our denomination right now?

15. What are your views on ———? (Choose any theological or social issues that are important in your congregation.)

16. Do you differ from the denomination's position on any theological issues? If so, what are they?

17. By what title do you prefer to be called?

18. (Name one of the problems identified through your

self-study.) How do you think you would go about trying to resolve it? (Do the same with other identified problems.)

19. How do you maintain your spiritual, emotional, and physical health? How do you like to spend your free time?

20. How do you allocate time to spend with your family?

21. What are your plans for continued personal and professional growth?

22.–25. Other specific questions for the applicant:

To spouse:

26. In what ways would you like to be involved in ministry, if any?

27. What is your attitude toward your husband's vocation?

28. Tell us about your children. Where are each of them in their faith pilgrimage?

29. What are your concerns about a possible move?

30. Are there any things about our church or community that would cause you apprehension if you were called to come here?

31.–32. Other specific questions for the spouse:

Give both an opportunity to ask questions of you.

If all committee members have read each finalist's PIF, have listened to two sermon tapes, and have been part of a group interview, you may not feel that visiting the candidate as a group in his home church is necessary. If you do not feel this is necessary, omitting it can save considerable committee time and expense. Omitting it also reduces the disruption that such a visit causes in the applicant's home church.

If your committee wishes to visit each applicant in his home church, schedule such a visit before, after, or simultaneously with this interview (i.e., have the interview in the afternoon following the Sunday morning service). Verify that the applicant will be preaching at his home church the day of your visit—one PNC drove from Iowa to Georgia to hear someone preach only to find that he'd scheduled a guest speaker for that day!

From these various sources of information—the PIF, the references, the sermons, and the personal interviews—you as a PNC probably will find that one candidate seems strongest to you when compared with your pastor profile. At this point prepare a verbal or written summary about this candidate, including the strengths you have identified, and give this statement to the board. With their approval, schedule a date for him to meet the congregation. It is appropriate at this time to ask the board or budget committee to prepare in writing the exact salary and benefit package (not just a range) that the church will offer to the applicant if the congregation calls him.

Presenting Candidates to the Congregation

Denominational leaders and pastors vary on the best way to present a candidate to the congregation. There is a consensus that PNCs should not present multiple candidates simultaneously to the congregation and have the congregation choose from among them. There the consensus stops. Let's look at some questions about which there are diverse answers.

First, how long should the candidate spend with the congregation? On the short end of the spectrum are those candidates who preach only one sermon Sunday morning and then the congregation votes to call or not to call. At the other end of the spectrum is Gerald Gillaspie, a pastor himself, who recommends that the candidating visit should extend over eight days, including two Sundays.[7]

Probably a single sermon, or even a single day, is too short a time for a pastor and a congregation to interact enough to know whether their expectations of each other are compatible. Eight days is too long for most pastors to take off from one church to candidate in another, especially since there is the possibility that they may not be called by that congregation.

A compromise would be for the pastor and his wife to spend from Wednesday evening through Sunday evening at the church where they are candidating. By using the days and evenings judiciously, they get an opportunity to interact with many congregation members and also see the community to consider whether they would feel comfortable there.

The church should pay for the candidate's meals, rooming, and mileage expenses during his stay—another reason a five-day visit may be better for the church than an eight-day visit.

Second, should he preach or not? Most churches have the candidate preach. Leonard Hill, a denominational leader in the Southern Baptist Convention, explains the rationale for *not* having the candidate preach:

> Some churches have discontinued having a prospective minister preach for the congregation before extending him a call. They prefer to base their final judgment on the report of the pulpit committee which has much more than simply hearing one or two sermons on which to base its report.[8]

We noted in chapter 1 that in the past many churches have made mistakes in choosing a pastor because they've overemphasized preaching skills, while preaching is only one portion of a pastor's work. When the congregation's only interaction with a candidate is hearing him preach one or two sermons, it's hard for them not to overemphasize preaching skills, for that is the only data they have on which to base their decision. Another alternative is to have the candidate preach but also interact with the congregation in ways that allow them to experience some of his pastoral skills.

Third, should the church vote on accepting or not accepting the candidate immediately or wait one week? Most congregational churches vote on a candidate the same Sunday that he preaches, usually while he waits in another part of the church. A congregation's anxiety is rapidly reduced if they can listen to someone preach, vote on him, and hear immediately his acceptance of their call. The candidate and his family do not have to endure the anxiety of waiting for a week before knowing the congregation's decision. This method also allows the candidate to return to his present congregation and resign before his congregation hears of his candidacy at another church through other sources.

However, Gerald Gillaspie states, "The church should never vote while the candidate is present nor on the same Sunday he candidates."[9] He does not give reasons for his prohibition, but perhaps we can suggest some. The candidating process has sometimes been compared to a dating situation, one in which the candidating pastor and the congregation are each checking the other out for compatibility. If in the excitement of each other's company they make a decision on whether to "marry," this decision is not likely to be as thoughtfully considered as one in which they separate for a week, use that week to think about what they've experienced in each other, and then decide.

Waiting a week could allow other problems to develop, however. For example, if one or more members or groups in the church have tried to exert control over the pastor, these individuals or groups could campaign for or against the candidate during the week. Such a situation could be allayed by an instruction from the board that there is to be no active campaigning during the week—each individual or couple should pray about the decision to be made and couples could discuss it together, then everyone should vote as he or she feels led without any attempts to influence other members' votes.

Obviously waiting a week before voting has advantages and disadvantages. Each PNC and board must make a decision about what seems the wisest course for their church to take.

Fourth, is there any way to ensure the candidate's confidentiality? Although securing the candidate's confidentiality may have been possible up to this point, the PNC can place few controls on the congregation after revealing his identity to them. The congregation can be asked to keep the candidate's identity in confidence, allowing him (if the church calls him) to tell his congregation that he is resigning. If the church does not call him, the congregation can be asked to keep this in confidence in order not to disrupt his present ministry.

Fifth (and probably most important), what kinds of activities should you schedule for the pastor, his spouse, and the church between Wednesday evening and Sunday? As with the farewell receptions for outgoing pastors, I think the social events that typically occur between Wednesday evening and Sunday do not make the best use of these important times.

The PNC can develop a one-page biographical introduction about the candidating pastor, summarizing his education, experience, and special gifts and qualities. The statement should include some of the reasons the PNC believes he is a good match for the church. Send this out in the latter part of the week before the candidate will visit the church, encouraging people to meet him on Wednesday night and at other events scheduled for that purpose. Then plan the use of Wednesday night through Sunday evening so that the pastor and his wife have an opportunity to meet a variety of people within the congregation. One or two people from the PNC could act as moderators for each meeting. In the meetings the candidate could be asked to describe his early life, his most influential teachers in school, college, and seminary, his pastoral experience and philosophy of leadership. His wife could be encouraged to share her thoughts about being a pastor's wife and the ministries that she enjoys. The church members can be encouraged to share how they have experienced the church and their hopes for its future. The moderator could encourage the pastor, his wife, and the congregational members to ask questions of each other. The tone of the meeting should be friendly getting-to-know-one-another rather than an interrogation. The PNC has already screened the pastor's application carefully for any negative qualities.

On Wednesday evening and Sunday morning the chair of the PNC or the board could introduce the candidate again, giving a synopsis of the information sent out in written form. On Sunday evening or a week later, a vote can be taken regarding the candidate. If the church extends a call, a contract specifying all the employment agreements, signed by the chair of the board or whoever has that authority, should accompany it. At this time make sure that all agreements discussed by the PNC and the candidate are confirmed in writing by those who will be responsible for carrying out those agreements.

If the congregation does not call your first candidate, wait at least two weeks before scheduling another candidate so that the congregation does not become overly fatigued. If your first candidate is rejected, the committee members should talk informally with congregational members to understand what caused the congregation to reject the candidate. Some things about the method of presenting the candidate may need to be adjusted. If you have correctly understood the needs of the church and the qualities of your applicants, the congregation will most likely affirm your first or second recommendation to them.

Bringing Closure to Your Work on the PNC

After you have found a candidate who has accepted the congregation's call, you will feel an enormous load lift from your shoulders. Your work is almost done. Here are a few remaining responsibilities. First, wait until you are sure that your candidate is coming. A few candidates, upon giving their resignations to their present congregations, have been greeted with such an outpouring of love and support that they decided to stay with the present congregation. That doesn't happen often, but it pays to wait until you are positive your candidate is coming before doing the following things.

Second, when you are certain that your new pastor is coming, send a personally addressed nonacceptance letter to each applicant to whom you have not already sent one (Appendix H has a sample letter). Third, send thank-you letters to all those people who helped in your pastoral search. Fourth, notify denominational officials that your vacancy has been filled. Fifth, have a debriefing time in which you as a committee talk about the various feelings you have experienced during this process and about what you have learned. You may wish to summarize the process you have used and what you have learned to leave as a legacy for the next nominating committee.

Sixth, with the board, plan how you will welcome your new pastor. The next chapter will give you several practical suggestions. Finally, have a dinner for committee members and spouses to celebrate the completion of this momentous task in the life of your church!

9

Welcoming the New Pastor and His Family

A Parable About Pastorate Start-Ups

A parable by Wm. Bud Phillips gives us several keen insights into the nature of a new pastorate start-up:

A certain actor, with experience and training, was offered a most challenging test by a wise director.

The actor was informed that he was to remain in the dressing room until the middle of the second act of a play he had never read or rehearsed. On a cue from the director, he was to walk on stage and begin to act.

At the appropriate time, the cue was given, and the actor entered stage left. At first the scenery bore a slight resemblance to a set in which he had played a starring role. He immediately assumed that role, but the other actors on stage seemed confused and even irritated. He soon fell silent. He then noticed that some of the actors appeared to be dressed in a costume similar to that used in another play in which he had had a major role. As he assumed that role, one of the actors left in disgust and another looked at him pityingly. After trying two or three other roles, familiar to him from the past, he concluded none of them quite suited the set, the costumes, or the lines being offered by the others on the stage.

He then "stepped out of character" and asked one of the actors if he could be told what was going on. The other actors gathered round and each told him something of what had been the play's action to the point of his entrance. "Well, what were you going to do when I came on stage?" he asked. "That's the strange thing," they said, "we didn't know what was to happen next." "Well, what am I supposed to do?" asked the actor. One of the members of the cast suggested an answer. "Perhaps with your experience and training you could help us find a satisfactory conclusion to the second act."

They then began to work at their new task, and the curtain remained up. They went back over the story as it had unfolded in the first act. They laughed and enjoyed the pleasure of remembering the mistakes they had made and the deeply emotional moments in the scenes that had led up to the arrival of the new actor. They examined the scenery and the staging plan and decided that there were some clues in the context to suggest some future direction. The experienced actor reminded them of some of the major themes of love, reconciliation, justice, peace, compassion, forgiveness, judgment and grace. The actors then took account of the people on stage and decided how they would continue to perform with some reshaping of their roles.

They suggested lines to each other, and together they began to interact to the delight of everyone.

The curtain fell to end the second act.

When the curtain went up again, all the actors were on stage except the one who had entered in the middle of the second act. The cast seemed puzzled and a little disorganized, and then there appeared from stage left another experienced and well-trained actor. At first she assumed the character of a number of roles she had played elsewhere, but the cast seemed confused and slightly irritated. Eventually, however. . . .[1]

As Phillips's parable suggests, pastors arrive on a stage where a drama has been unfolding for some time. They usually have little information about the preceding story or the characters, although the congregation expects them to immediately take a leading role. They sometimes begin acting based on similarities they detect between the present situation and situations they have been in before. However, they often find that those former roles are not compatible with the needs and expectations of persons in the present situation.

Pastorate Start-Ups as "Dangerous Opportunities"

Roy Oswald has said, "Each pastorate start up should be viewed as 'a dangerous opportunity.'"[2] A new pastorate has all the potential and excitement of a new romance. It also contains dangers. The new pastor does not know most of the expectations of his new congregation. He does not know the sociological mores of that particular congregation. He can, therefore, unwittingly alienate his congregation even though his intentions are to be caring and concerned. His new pastorate is filled with "land mines" about which he must be warned.

Books for Your New Pastor

To be successful a new pastor must avoid the "land mines" and also "join" with the congregation and staff. Only in the last few years has any writing focused on these two tasks. The Alban Institute, based in Washington D.C., has been a leader in developing these materials. The institute has published several books, booklets, and essays regarding pastoral endings, pastoral searches, and pastorate start-ups. Here are some short books I recommend purchasing for your new pastor to help him make the transition to your church most successfully:

1. *New Beginnings: A Pastorate Start Up Workbook* by Roy M. Oswald,

2. *Pastoral Transitions: From Endings to New Beginnings* by Wm. Bud Phillips, and

3. *The Pastor as Newcomer* by Roy M. Oswald.

You can reach the Alban Institute at 1-800-457-2674.

Making a Leadership Change: How Organizations and Leaders Can Handle Leadership Transitions Successfully, by Thomas Gilmore, is an excellent secular book with much useful information for pastors in new churches. The section from pages 107 to 261 is especially relevant for pastors changing churches.

The books just mentioned give pastors information about their approach to change. Since I am writing this book to and for church members, I will focus my comments on what you can do to help your new pastor and his family feel welcome and therefore help them "join" with your congregation. These suggestions come from two main sources: pastors giving ideas about what congregations can do to help new pastors feel welcome, and books describing the process of a new leader's joining a group.

Renounce Unrealistic Hopes

We need to recognize our secret hopes and renounce our unrealistic ones. Roy Oswald remarks, "Each [PNC] member harbors a secret hope that you [the new pastor] will walk on water and bring such energy and vitality to the parish that they will have to hold people back at the door. (They may not admit this openly, but they all hope they will be remembered as the group that made a super choice for the parish.)"[3] PNC members need to recognize and renounce this secret hope so that the new pastor is free to be human and fallible.

Develop a Transition Team

Create a transition team whose purpose is to help the incoming pastor make a successful transition to his new church. I would recommend that the transition team be composed of three or four members from the PNC and the same number from the church board. Having six to eight members allows the team to address many different areas without a great burden falling on any individual. The transition team can coordinate all the suggested activities discussed in the remainder of this chapter or at least all the activities that you believe would be appropriate for your congregation.

Activities Before Your Pastor's Arrival

Begin Building Relationships Early

The psychological bond between the new pastor and the congregation can start to form even before he arrives. The transition team can publish the pastor's present home address and encourage church members to write notes to him and his family. These notes can be short, just letting the pastor's family know the congregation is looking forward to their coming and is praying for them. The transition team also can ask the pastor and his wife what kinds of information would be most helpful for them to gather. The team can find out the costs of moving and make sure that the church pays for as much of them as possible. The incoming pastor can be encouraged to write a "pastoral letter" that can be distributed to the congregation before his arrival.[4]

The PNC can talk with the pastor and his family enough to know what they appreciate and need. For example, some introverted pastors may prefer a small reception or a series of small receptions rather than a large one. The committee can ask the wife her preferences for colors and wallpaper in various rooms of the parsonage. The committee can make certain that the parsonage and the pastor's study are clean, fixed up, and repainted.

Provide Help with Housing

If the church does not provide a parsonage, the committee can tell the pastor's family about the various school districts and help them locate a good Realtor. Especially if the pastor must buy his first house, this issue is important. Oswald observes, "Pastors are very poorly prepared for the process of moving from a parsonage into a house they have purchased. Assign someone to help them with this."[5]

Even if the pastor has purchased a house before, the transition team can be helpful. Sometimes a pastor and his family are unable to make the down payment on a home in your community until their previous home sells. Or if this is their first home, they may not have the money for a down payment. In either instance some churches have agreed to lend them the money for the down payment. This amount can be repaid when the pastor's previous home sells. If there was no previous home, some churches "forgive" a certain portion of the loan each year that the pastor continues his ministry at that church.

Once the pastor and his wife have decided on a location, the transition team can make a map for the places the family needs to go and how long it takes to get there. These can include shopping centers, supermarkets, dentists, doctors, mechanics, hairdressers, and so on.[6]

Plan for the Wife's Ministry

The transition team can find out the wife's talents and desires for service. They can help work out possible problems if others are already doing these things. If the wife lacks leadership talent or is too busy with other work, they can make certain the church realizes that it hired her husband and not her.[7]

Acquaint the Pastor with the Church's Present Ministries

During the interim period the transition team should ask each ministry head to develop material about the status of the ministry with which to brief the new pastor. Include budget, current expenses in comparison to the budget, key personnel, strengths, and problems needing attention eventually or immediately.

Establish a Personnel Committee

If the church does not have a personnel committee, recommend that the board establish one. The purpose of this committee is to engage in community research that helps keep church workers' salaries and benefits comparable to those of the local community. They can help the pastor develop job descriptions and personnel policies and search for the best insurance and other benefit programs for church staff. A pastor should not have to ask for a raise. The personnel committee should take the initiative in providing cost-of-living adjustments and raises that reflect the quality of the pastor's ministry.

Some churches that welcome a new pastor are unable to pay salaries at the level they wish. One pastor suggested several things that they can do in such a situation. They can say, "We know you are worth more, but we can't afford it now." They also can give perquisites that don't cost the church much, such as another week of vacation, a six-month or one-year anniversary party, or a book allowance.

Send Pictures

If your church has a pictorial directory, send a copy to the new pastor, identifying currently active people. If you have a packet of information that tells about your current ministries (such as one given to first-time attenders), send it with the pictorial directory.

Introduce Children to Peers

The transition team should identify several families willing to introduce the children to others in their age group, both at school and at church. Others can take responsibility for introducing the pastor and his wife to various community groups in which they have an interest.

On moving day the transition committee can make sure

there are people at the pastor's new home to welcome the family and help them move in. Some churches, especially when the church cannot afford to pay professional movers, have even sent a team to help the pastor and his family load their truck and help them drive to their new community.

The transition team can plan the formal welcome or installation service. The service can be led by a denominational official, with components that both welcome the pastor and his family and underscore the meaning of this step in the congregation's spiritual life. Anthony Plathe asserts, "When the beginning of a ministry is ritualized, its importance may be more fully appreciated."[8]

Activities at the Time of Your Pastor's Arrival

Give Your Pastor a "Pounding"

Several pastors mentioned a tradition that meant a great deal to them as they moved into a new congregation. The tradition is called a pounding or pantry shower. Finding the pantry stocked with many staples they will need for the next six months is a meaningful expression of love for many pastors' families, especially when they are often grieving the loss of relationships from their former congregation.

Make a Big Deal of Welcoming Them

Pastors mentioned that when a new congregation "goes the extra mile" in helping them on moving day, the effort means a lot. Some transition teams put up signs at the church and at the parsonage welcoming the new pastor and his family. Some teams arrange for a local newspaper to interview him, or they write an article to submit to the newspaper.

Provide Child Care and Meals

If the pastor has small children, some teams provide child care during the first several days after the move. Often teams ask different families to prepare supper for the first week. Some churches arrange for families with children the same ages as the pastor's to host the pastor's children during the first week or two so that they can start to build friendships. The pastor and his wife have an immediate identity at the new church, but their children do not. Pastors remarked regularly in my interviews that they especially appreciated the congregation's efforts to help the children feel accepted and become involved with their new peer groups.

Plan a Meaningful Installation Service

The transition team can arrange to have the pastor spend his first Sunday in his new congregation sitting in the pew. He can move in without the pressure of preparing for a service and also observe the present worship patterns customary for the congregation.[9]

Church consultant Loren Mead echoes the sentiments of Anthony Plathe about the significance of embodying the welcome and installation service within a religious ritual:

> Installation into the community, congregation, the ecumenical world, and the judicatory calls for the best that a congregation can do in its life of liturgy and worship. Whatever the heritage of the congregation, it should use that fully and well in "showing off" its new pastor, celebrating a new chapter in the work of the congregation. We encourage congregations to pull out all the stops. Pastors of other congregations and lay leaders should be invited to participate.
>
> The installation is not a personal event—it is an event having to do with a congregation's entry into a new phase of its life and ministry. It is also a statement of hope about what life is to be and a statement of invitation to others to be with them in their journey.[10]

Among other things, the installation service might include reciting of commitments or covenants the congregation make to their new pastor and reciprocal commitments he makes to them. The installation service can be followed by a fellowship dinner for the congregation that expresses their happiness about his coming.

Have an Orientation to the Church Facilities

After the pastor has moved in and is somewhat settled, one or more persons from the transition team can conduct an orientation to the facilities, the office, and current church procedures. Things that look simple to old-timers may bewilder someone new.[11]

Introduce Pastor to Key Community Leaders

Anthony Plathe suggests, "Introduce the pastor to the congregation and leaders of the community. Some people are gregarious and outgoing, while others find meeting new people difficult. Having a local person help with introductions can greatly speed up the welcoming process."[12]

Activities During the First Month After Your Pastor's Arrival

Encourage Pastor and Family to Take Time to Grieve

Most pastors move immediately from one congregation to another, usually with no vacation or break in between. A few pastors take a one-week break between congregations. Most pastors are grieving the loss of the former congregation, their associates, and their community friends while they are trying to become oriented to a new congregation. Most pastors don't talk with new congregation members about their grief, believing that doing so might suggest a lack of enthusiasm about the new congregation.

Unexpressed grief can affect a pastor's productiveness, his level of motivation, and his ability to establish new relationships. It may even cause him to wonder whether he should have taken the new church. A transition team can recognize their new pastor may be grieving and encourage him to spend extra time with his family (who are also grieving) during this period. He may benefit from talking about this issue with a denominational official who understands those feelings.

Allow Pastor to "Join" with All the Subgroups in the Church

The pastor can "join" with the staff and congregational members by affirming the healthy parts of the congregational life while simultaneously empathizing with the pain of the less-healthy parts. As he lets people tell their stories he gives them some hope that he can help them in the places where they are "stuck," and they sense that he is "joining" with them. He needs to acknowledge their present structure and leadership before he attempts any changes. He should avoid getting permanently caught in a coalition with one party or another but should move to connect with different groups so that each group feels understood.[13]

Each of these things helps him "join" with his new staff and congregation. The transition team can aid this process by encouraging him to spend this time hearing various groups and individuals and not demanding that he empathize only with their positions and perspectives.

Allow your pastor to be a "student" awhile. He knows much less about the congregation than do many members and the present staff. Asking questions does many things simultaneously. It enables the pastor to learn about the congregation rapidly. It shows that he wants to understand the present system and not just impose his system on the congregation without understanding it first. It helps him avoid making mistakes that could alienate some members. It increases the respect of the staff and congregation for him; his thoughtful questions convince them of his wisdom and his respect for their present efforts.

177

Don't Expect New Programs Immediately

Give up expectations that your new pastor immediately begin new programs. Roy Oswald states,

> We are convinced that the most important question people have when they first meet their new pastor is: "Will this pastor like me and will this pastor care for me?" . . . This is why we feel so strongly that clergy new to their congregation should spend six to nine months being little more than a lover and a historian. It's hard work getting to know almost everyone and finding something you can love them for. When all the energy goes into changing the parish around, this outreach will get little attention. The long-term effects can be costly.[14]

The transition team can encourage congregational members to have the pastor and his family into their homes for a meal or to take them out to a restaurant. Many pastors mentioned that a congregation made them feel welcome in this way.

Help Him Learn Your Church's History

Your new pastor understands some of your church's history and expectations from your self-study. However, go over this material again since anxiety and the intervening period of saying good-bye to his former church may have clouded his memory of this information. Roy Oswald observes,

> In starting up a ministry in a new parish, it is our experience that paying attention to those portions of history that people remember and pass on is very important. In the first place, it gets clergy beyond the arrogant assumption that nothing of significance has happened in this parish till they arrived. Secondly, it puts them in touch with the hopes and expectations of the congregation.[15]

Management Design, Inc., has developed an excellent way to help a pastor become aware of historical events in the church's past. The pastor invites a group of people from the congregation to join him for an evening or a Saturday afternoon of historical recollection and reflection. He should try to contract for three and one-half to four hours together.

The pastor begins by pasting several large sheets of newsprint on the wall and drawing a horizontal line through the middle of the sheets. At the right end of the sheets, draw a vertical line and label it "the present." During the first hour, have the group start at the present and work backward, recording on the newsprint the historical events that they remember. (This should be done without reference to any written documents.)

During the second hour, the group should develop "meaning statements" as a way of explaining the psychological significance of these historical events for themselves and for the congregation. The group should answer the question: What meaning do these events, individually and together, have for us and our church?

During the third hour, urge each person to select a meaning statement that is particularly significant for him or her. Ask each one to explain why it is personally significant and what commitment he or she is willing to make to continue that norm, value, or activity in the future. By doing this the incoming pastor has an idea of some commitments of specific members to various areas of ministry.[16]

Recognize Oscillation Is Normal

Whenever there is a pastoral change, some oscillation occurs. The previous pastor attracted certain congregational members to him, and they were highly involved in the ministries of the church. They may be tired at the time of a pastoral change, and some may decide to take a needed rest.

Others have been uninvolved in the church ministries during the tenure of the former pastor. They may decide that they want to be more involved in ministry, or they may be attracted to the new pastor for a variety of reasons, so they volunteer.

This change—of heavily involved people becoming less active and of less involved people becoming more active—is called oscillation.[17] When several of their most active laypersons become less active at the time of a pastoral change, congregations need not fear that the church is dying; this experience normally accompanies pastoral change.

Understand the Subgroups within a Congregation

Wm. Bud Phillips has identified eight subsystems or subgroups in most congregations: (1) those who are primarily concerned with the worship and celebration aspects of the church; (2) those who are most concerned about the nurture of Christian education in the church; (3) those who are most concerned about having fellowship, making newcomers feel welcome, and visiting the sick; (4) those who are most committed to trying to restore persons who are lonely or offended or fearful; (5) those who are concerned with the maintenance and stability of the congregation and the church buildings; (6) those who are transient and do not expect to be with the church a long time; (7) those who are primarily concerned about evangelism; and (8) those who are primarily concerned that the church reach out to the poor and otherwise disadvantaged.

Messages from people in these various subsystems can be confusing to the new pastor, who may believe that each represents a significant-sized group in the congregation. A pastor should not act on a suggestion from a person in one subgroup until he has a sense of its priority for the entire congregation. Congregation members should give a new pastor time to understand the size of each subgroup and not try to pressure him into acting on their particular agenda.[18]

Help Your Pastor Minimize Taxes

A transition team can ask an accountant to meet with the new pastor and help him develop a way of defining his salary and expenses that maximizes the taxation benefits applied to clergy. This practice is not illegal or unethical. The federal government has adopted certain measures that apply to the taxation of clergy, and there is no reason not to take advantage of these measures.

The First Six Months After the Move

Provide a Date a Month

Pastors suggested several ways that congregational members can make them feel welcome during the first six months of their pastorate. One suggestion was for the church to arrange twelve nights out during the first year. On each night the church furnishes and pays for a sitter.

Give Honest Feedback

Another suggestion was to give honest feedback, something beyond "That was a great message!" The feedback can be either positive or negative. Pastors, as do other leaders, appreciate it when members carefully think through negative feedback before giving it. Pastors say they feel accepted when congregational members allow them to minister to them and when they are supportive of new programs pastors introduce.

Protect Your New Pastor from Ongoing Feuds

The transition team can protect the new pastor by trying to prevent individuals from attempting to enlist the pastor's support in an ongoing feud. The board can address ongoing conflicts during the interim through various problem-solving activities. These activities may involve the interim pastor, an outside consultant, or some conflict resolution work done by the board. It is hardly fair to the new pastor if the board has not done all it can to cause resolution before he comes.

At the beginning of a pastorate a new pastor's authority is at its weakest. Confronting a strongly embedded coalition in the first few months of a new pastorate can result in a premature termination. Since the problem preceded the pastor, he is not its cause. Therefore, the board should attempt to resolve the problem before a new pastor arrives rather than wait and expect the new pastor to resolve it.

However, even when the board or PNC attempts to do this, there will undoubtedly be times when a problem remains unresolved. In this event the PNC should have alerted the candidating pastor to the problem, and he should have indicated his willingness to come anyway. After his arrival at the new church, the transition team should inform him of unresolved conflicts or problematic persons. The new pastor can most easily avoid getting into a conflict if he knows about it and its players beforehand. Those who present the issues and identify the individuals involved should try to do so in an objective manner.

Long-Term Ways of Expressing Caring

Provide for Continued Professional Growth

Pastors offered several suggestions in this area. One was for the church to set aside an amount of money in the budget for continuing education. To a pastor this says, "We believe you are a person worth investing in."

Remember His Family

Pastors also mentioned remembering the family. For example, on his wife's birthday the church might give her a dozen roses. Or on their anniversary, the church might give them a gift certificate to a nice restaurant. Some congregations celebrate a Pastor's Appreciation Day on the anniversary of his coming.

The following essay by Cliff Stabler is the best article I have ever read on long-term ways of showing love to a pastor. I will close this chapter by quoting it in its entirety.[19]

The Care and Feeding of Shepherds

Our parsonage was a rented two-story farmhouse with no plumbing and no central heat. The church my father served in rural Illinois needed but could not support a full-time shepherd. So he also drove school buses and sold men's clothing at Ward's.

Christmas could have been a cold and hungry time had it not been for the Christian love and sharing of our parishioners. It was their practice to bring forty or fifty bushels of food to the church the Sunday night just before Christmas. Our whole family would stand in the front of the sanctuary and receive these love-gifts with tears of appreciation streaming down our faces. That annual event was the care and feeding of their shepherd.

Years later, with an unmistakable call to serve as a committed layman, I found myself in a position to minister to the needs of spiritual shepherds. And I discovered that there was much to learn about this responsibility.

It was a significant step when I learned that the shepherd-flock analogy had its limitations. Correcting this to the concept of co-workers in Christ freed me to minister to my pastor's needs as well as to be ministered to by him. This co-worker had been given specialized functions or "gifts" to be used in the Body of Christ, just as the Lord had given some to me. Each of us was called to a particular role. The pastor serves as an equipper and enabler of co-workers who carry out the ministry in various ways.

I realized that this co-worker was also a co-struggler. His condition of redeemed sinner was no different than mine. Both of us stood before the grace of God—trying, failing, sometimes succeeding in being faithful to our calling. This realization enabled me to treat him as a fellow human being, rather than as a "house Christian" to be called upon to say grace at special functions.

Accepting my pastor as a fellow struggler meant that I tried to treat him the way I wanted him to treat me. I avoided condemning him when he did not live up to my high expectations of him. I did not expect him to be more than I was willing to be myself. And, most importantly, I sought to minister to him rather than merely waiting for him to minister to me. Here are some of the forms my ministry to him took (not listed in any order):

1. occasionally inviting him to play tennis, or to sit around and talk;

2. believing in him, his potential, his promise, and thanking God for what He has done and is going to do in the pastor's life;

3. believing in other Christians and affirming God's grace in their lives (this serves as food to the pastor, because he finds meaning in his life by the spiritual growth he observes in his congregation);

4. trying to sense his needs before they become pressing (for example, suggesting that he be given a raise before he has to ask for it);

5. following through in my responsibility or finding a fellow layman to do it rather than dumping a job on the pastor;

6. insisting that he spend times of rest and vacation with his family, and not with members of the congregation;

7. listening to him and meeting him where he is by extending myself as I really am, not as I want him to think I am;

8. realizing that he has hundreds of names to remember when he stumbles over mine;

9. being aware that there are moments when he needs the truth, not tact—the truth spoken in love, not hostility, and motivated by his need, not by my insecurities;

10. expecting him to be a student of God's Word;

11. trying to turn his vision and thoughts to Jesus Christ when he is discouraged and cynical or overburdened and weary;

12. facilitating reconciliation between him and any in the congregation with whom he is estranged;

13. forgetting the weight and burden of his schedule when he can be used, for that is his life-blood.

If he is a husband and father, I can minister further to him:

1. Realize that the congregation did not hire his wife and children. She does not have to be an officer of any group or even a member of it. She does not have to teach Sunday school or sing in the choir just because she is the pastor's wife.

2. Treat their children as I treat the other children in the congregation, with neither more nor less deference, no more critical an attitude.

3. Honor the privacy of their personal lives. How his wife keeps their house and spends her time is their business. Where they go on vacation and how much it costs is their business. How often they mow the grass and trim the hedge is their business.

4. Pray for them always.

It is exciting to discover ways of taking part in the care and feeding of shepherds. The love, affirmation, and ministry of parishioners may lead a pastor to feel as Paul did toward the congregation at Philippi: "I thank my God for you all every time I think of you; and every time I pray for you, I pray with joy, because of the way in which you have helped me in the work of the gospel, from the very first day until now" (Phil. 1:3–5, Good News for Modern Man).

10

What to Do When Conflict Develops

Whenever two or more people are in a relationship, conflict will eventually develop because we all have expectations of others. Sometimes we verbalize our expectations; more frequently we do not. When someone in a relationship fails to meet one of our expectations, we are likely to become frustrated. Perhaps we expected someone to do something that he didn't do, or maybe we expected someone not to do something that she did do. That happens whether our expectations are realistic or unrealistic.

Most conflicts in a church eventually focus on the pastor, whether or not they started there. We all come to church with many expectations of what we want our pastor to be. Conflict often begins when he fails to meet the expectations of one or more congregational members. However, sometimes conflict develops between two persons or groups within the congregation. If he sides with one group, he immediately antagonizes the other. If he tries to remain neutral, both groups (and possibly the entire congregation) may become angry with him for not having sided with them or for not having resolved the conflict. If he tries to actively resolve the conflict and the two groups decide that they will not make peace, the congregation may consider the pastor ineffective and powerless because of his failure. Thus even if the stubbornness of congregational members causes the pastor to fail in his attempt to resolve the conflict, the pastor is likely to be blamed.

The seminary curriculum rarely touches on congregational or personal conflict resolution. Although there was plenty of conflict in the early Christian church, only a rudimentary plan of congregational conflict management is given in Scripture (see Matt. 18:15–17). Most churches are unprepared to deal with significant conflict. Church consultant Speed Leas says, "I have not yet been in a church that has a decent set of understandings of how to deal with differences when they arise."[1]

Though a growing consensus among church consultants from a variety of denominations is that longer pastorates (between eight and twelve years) are healthier for everyone involved,[2] several factors work against achieving them. As mentioned in an earlier chapter, the "winning coach" mentality views leaders as disposable if the home team (church) isn't doing as well as the fans think it should. The trend to leave relationships rather than stay in them and try to resolve problems is occurring not just in marriages but also in the workplace. A. O. Hirschman remarks, "Loyalty is weaker, and people are more likely to resolve conflicts by exiting rather than staying to work through their issues."[3] Thus even though there is the recognition that longer pastorates are healthier, cultural factors and congregational conflict often lead to brief pastorates.

How Does Conflict Unfold?[4]

Congregational conflict can be described in four stages. Stage one contains *early warning signs,* such as increased complaining and withdrawal of contact between certain groups or between persons and the pastor. There is likely to be a decline in attendance and giving, and those who have been faithful lay leaders for years may gradually resign. Another early warning sign is the emergence of "hard-liners," people taking adamant stands on issues rather than being willing to compromise. Changes are likely in the pastor's behavior as he attempts to adjust to the increased tension within the congregation.

Stage two has been called *the cold shoulder in a room of rumors*. People indirectly display their anger by conspicuously avoiding greeting certain people. They intentionally make others feel uncomfortable and rejected by their silence at times when conversation would be appropriate. People start to circulate petitions demanding the resignation of the pastor, but the antagonists are unwilling to talk about the issues openly with those with whom they disagree.

Stage three has been called *jumping to conclusions*. The conclusion is usually that the solution to the problem is to get rid of someone (generally the pastor). This conclusion is usually premature because the parties have not clearly identified the issues, they have not attempted to see if changes could occur between them, and neither party has clearly shown that removal of one or more persons would solve the problem.

Stage four is *decision making*. The congregation makes a decision, usually to remove the pastor. In a congregational church the congregation can do this without approval from anyone else. In a connectional church approval from a denominational executive may be required. Sometimes the denominational executive will not approve such an action until there has been some attempt to clarify the issues and work on them.

Understanding Dissatisfaction with Pastors Developmentally

During the first few years (especially the first two years), several developmental changes take place in the relationship between a pastor and his congregation. Most of these processes occur at a subconscious or an unconscious level. (I am using these two terms with slightly different meanings. By subconscious I am referring to processes about which persons are not consciously aware but they can quickly recognize once the processes have been explained to them. The processes occurring during the honeymoon period are subconscious; most people would immediately verify their existence once they are explained. The processes I will describe that follow the honeymoon period are unconscious processes; that is, most people must think about their relationships for some time before they can recognize them.)

The "honeymoon period" lasts anywhere from six to eighteen months. The new pastor is the recipient of much congregational affection. People frequently take him and his family out to eat or invite them into their homes. People send him cards telling him how happy they are that he is their pastor. Members give gifts at birthdays and anniversaries and Christmas. Members or staff write letters to the state headquarters telling of the way God is blessing the church. Members encourage him to take care of his health.

Church consultant Roy Oswald thinks that discussing the honeymoon period as if it were one continuing process is inaccurate. He also believes that although the surface behavior of congregational members suggests that all is well, some processes happening under the surface are not always positive. He explains,

Talk about the "honeymoon" period in this situation is confusing. Are people talking about the time in which parish and pastor live together harmoniously because they are living out of their projections and hopes? Or about the time in which each withholds honest feedback from the other? It is almost as though there are two phases to the honeymoon period. The first is a relatively short period of time, one to four weeks, in which each functions out of unreal data about the other. There is a sense in which new objects are overvalued (ministers, babies, a new spouse, etc.). We project onto the other our hopes and dreams of what we would like him/her to be. In pastorate start ups, the clay feet of both the pastor and parish are exposed very quickly. We discovered, in our research with the Army Chaplain's Board, that people need a minimum of two contacts to arrive at a realistic assessment of the new chaplain.

There is a second period which follows: one during which people withhold their candor from the new clergyperson. It is as though parishioners contract with one another to suspend judgment until the new minister is given a fair chance, or until they have an opportunity to get to know him/her better. On the surface it seems as though everything is going well. Clergy can fall into the trap and construe this seeming harmony as approval for what they are doing. In this sense, congregations give new clergy enough rope to hang themselves. Some clergy continue to "do their thing," assuming the parish will tell them if they disapprove. They alienate themselves from some and lose the confidence of others. When the period of testing is over, they have come up with a poor grade.[5]

Warner White has also written about developmental processes of the first few years of a pastorate.[6] These processes probably occur at an unconscious rather than a subconscious level, and some would deny that they occur at all. White believes that each process produces a measure of conflict but that a pastor should not leave his church because of it. He believes the conflict produced by these processes is an important part of the spiritual growth of church members.

The first developmental process is that people come to know their pastor not only as a symbol of God but also as a fallible human being. The gap between the pastor as a priest and the pastor as a fallible human being represents a serious scandal to many congregation members. They hope and want their pastor to be more than any human being can be, and their disappointment when they find out he is merely human is deep. Some members become angry and remain so. Such anger is difficult to deal with, and sometimes pastors are tempted to leave a church because of it.

A second developmental change that White talks about is the normal set of changes in the pastoral bond. Married persons go through three stages of love—illusion, disillusion, and realistic love. Love before marriage often is based on illusion—based more on the lovers' hopes of what they will receive from the partner than on what the partner can realistically give. In the first years of marriage both partners experience a gradual disillusionment. Each person develops a more realistic picture of the other and of what the partner can give. If they stay together and continue working on their relationship, they will enter a period of realistic love where they know what they can give and receive from each other and become content with that.

The relationship between a pastor and his congregation also goes through a sequence of illusion, disillusion, and realistic love. During the second part of the honeymoon period, the disillusionment process occurs although the pastor may not be aware of that because he receives no negative feedback. If his behavior is too unacceptable to the congregation, the disillusionment becomes so great that when the congregation does start to give him honest feedback his relationship with them is beyond repair. Pastors who do not behave unacceptably will experience some conflict during the disillusionment period. However, if they remain with the church, they will enter a period of realistic love and productive life with the congregation.

Third, White suggests that there are three stages in the development of healthy respect. The first stage is that of adoration, a strong word that captures the intensity with which many congregational members revere their new pastor. As they become aware of his humanness and fallibility, they enter a period of disappointment. If both pastor and congregation continue to work on the relationship, the result will be an attitude of respect. The respect includes a recognition that the pastor is a fallible human being, that he is also wise and caring, and that God has called him to an office meriting respect.

Fourth is the developmental process regarding power. In the first stage, members are often willing to trust their new pastor to such a degree that they become overly dependent on him to make decisions about the church. Even before the new pastor arrives, members begin deferring decisions, wanting the new pastor to be able to set the direction for the church. After he arrives and as they become more aware of his humanness (especially if they have difficulty adjusting to certain parts of his personality), they may enter a period of counterdependence. During this period, they may disagree with the pastor on issues based on their unconscious need to differentiate themselves from him. In the third stage, the congregation and the pastor enter a period of interdependence. Each recognizes the wisdom and perspectives of the other, and they realize that they can do more by listening to each other and cooperating than by opposing each other.

White indicates that some conflicts pastors experience with their congregations in the first few years represent a working through of these four developmental processes. A fifth cause of conflict may be the residual effects from a previous pastorate. When any of these is the reason for conflict, White encourages pastors to remain with the congregation and work through the problem. In my interviews with pastors and denominational leaders, several indicated that pastors who stay and work through the difficulties that typically arise between the first eighteen to thirty-six months of a pastorate usually experience the richest times of their ministry after this period. Many pastors leave between eighteen and twenty-four months into a pastorate because of conflict with the congregation. Leaving at this point means they never have an opportunity to experience the most satisfying part of a pastoral relationship.

Why Are Pastors Fired?

In the early 1980s an interdenominational group under the direction of Rev. Speed Leas conducted a study of 128 situations in which congregations had fired their pastors. They excluded from their study situations in which there had been a moral lapse so that they could investigate situations in which the reason for the firing was less clear.[7]

Professional incompetence was a reason for a congregation firing a pastor in 6 to 13 percent of the churches. The most frequent component noted in this category was incompetence in church administration. Other factors noted with some frequency included inability to communicate clearly verbally or in writing, inability to counsel, inability to make a professional call, and incompetence in the planning and implementation of celebration and worship.

Interpersonal incompetence was a much more frequent reason for termination than professional incompetence. In 23 percent of the churches studied, the congregation fired the pastor because he was too passive, withdrawn, distant, or cold, or he seemed not to care. In another 23 percent of the churches, the church fired the pastor for being too aggressive (i.e., contentious, authoritarian, or dictatorial). Thus in nearly 50 percent of the congregations that fired their pastors, the major reason was either interpersonal passivity or aggressiveness.

Congregational factors were prominent in 43 percent of the situations where congregations fired their pastors (that was the analysis of the researchers, not necessarily the reason those congregations would give if asked). In those congregations one or more of the following factors were present:

- a congregational history of firing pastors,
- factions within the congregation, often that went back many years,
- disapproval by a powerful minority of any person (including the pastor) who attempted to broaden the decision-making power base of the congregation, and
- a history of unwillingness to identify problems when they were small and work on them.

Although this discussion has tried to identify primary reasons for involuntary terminations, the investigators concluded that usually a variety of factors were involved. Both congregation and pastor contributed to the outcome. In their words "we could find few situations that were all the congregation's 'fault,' [and] we could find few that were all the pastor's 'fault.'"

Levels of Conflict

Speed Leas has modified the work of Malcolm Leary[8] and developed a helpful model for understanding the levels of conflict that can be present in a church situation. Within each level the key identifying characteristics are the parties' objectives and the way they use language.[9]

Level 1: Problems to Solve

At Level 1, people's objective is to solve the problem in a way that respects the needs and values of everyone involved. They share information openly with one another and believe that through collaboration they can find a workable solution. They make an effort to include everyone in the discussions. They try to use rational methods to decide what is wrong and how to fix it. Statements are problem oriented, not person oriented.

Level 2: Disagreement

At Level 2, the objective shifts from problem resolution to self-protection. There is still the desire to solve the problem but to do so without harming one's position or reputation. People at Level 2 call friends to discuss the problem and plan strategy.

People at Level 2 no longer use specific names for individuals. They view those who want something different from what they do as a group and refer to them as a group rather than as individuals. (It seems easier psychologically to plan strategy against others if we no longer think of them as persons, but emotionally distance ourselves from them through an impersonal group label.)

In Level 2, people begin to be less open about sharing information that would help the group reach a solution. Level 2 members share only the information that they believe will not hurt their position. They may resort to passive-aggressive (hostile) humor.

Level 3: Contest

In Level 3, we see the introduction of win/lose dynamics. The objective of Level 3 is not problem resolution (as in Level 1) or problem resolution and self-protection (as in Level 2), but winning. Usually more than one issue is at stake, and people begin to polarize around these issues (i.e., factions are born).

In Level 3, people begin to perceive the world in distorted ways, such as the following:

- *Magnification*—the tendency to see oneself as better than one really is and those on the other side as more evil than they really are.
- *Dichotomization*—the tendency to divide issues and people into two polarized categories (right and wrong) without recognizing that many issues and arguments provide a range of choices.
- *Overgeneralization*—the tendency to magnify the opponent's frequency of doing negative things and reduce the frequency of doing positive things (e.g., "You always. . . ," "You never . . .").
- *Mind reading*—people believe they can read their opponent's mind and motives.

In Level 3 conflict, people misperceive reality and resort to irrational thinking. For example, they frequently state conclusions that do not follow from the data. They may exaggerate ideas, data, or incidents in ways that will strengthen their case.

At Level 3, there is a resistance to peace overtures. Attacks on persons are frequent rather than a focus on solving problems. People use emotional attacks and appeals more frequently than appeals to reason. People are committed to "winning" rather than to working out a solution that respects the needs and feelings of everyone.

Level 4: Fight or Flight

At this level, the contestants' goals change from wanting to win to wanting to hurt or get rid of the other party. Unlike Level 3 behavior, where the goal is to force the others to change, at this point contestants no longer believe the others can or will change. The only option is to remove the other person (or group) from the environment. Each group wants to be right and punish the other group.

At this level, factions solidify, and each subgroup sees its continuation as more important than the health and continuation of the total organization. People in one group emotionally detach from those in the other group, which allows them to block out their awareness of the pain they are causing those in the other group. They often develop a self-righteous, unforgiving coldness toward them.

Level 5: Intractable Situations

The goal of participants in a Level 4 conflict is to punish others or remove them from the organization. In a Level 5 conflict, the objective is to *destroy* the others. Members view the opposition as unhealthy for the organization and harmful to society at large; therefore, it must be removed. A group operating at Level 5 not only would seek to remove a pastor from their church but would attempt to keep him from ever pastoring in any church again.

When a group has reached this level of hostility, it has lost a sense of reality, of God's compassion, and of the biblical themes of confession and restoration. Group members are no longer in control of their anger; it controls them. They remind one of Frederic Farrar's description of the dogmatic quarrels of European believers during the 1600s: Farrar remarked that those Christians "read the Bible by the unnatural glare of theological hatred."[10]

Results of Firing a Pastor

Three researchers, Fink, Beak, and Taddeo, have described the usual stages an organization goes through in attempting to recover from a crisis. The four stages are (1) shock, (2) defensive retreat, (3) acknowledgment, and (4) adaptation and change.

Speed Leas's research group found strong evidence that even twelve to twenty-four months after a pastor's termination many congregations were still "stuck" in the defensive retreat stage. Here is some of their evidence:

- Eighty-three percent of the congregations contacted refused to participate in the research project.
- Identification of people in camps or factions.
- Guarded communication across factional lines.
- Rivalry between groups in the congregation.
- Autocratic control by the new pastor or a continuing leadership group within the congregation.
- Preoccupation with maintenance and survival rather than the larger purposes of the church.
- Hopelessness, powerlessness, and lifelessness on the part of most members (especially the leaders).
- Lack of experimentation with new ideas for program and development.
- Dull and constricted worship; dull and constricted meetings and programs.
- Dwindling participation of members.
- Dwindling financial giving by members.[11]

The Importance of Having a Model of Congregational Conflict Resolution

Earlier in this chapter Speed Leas was quoted as saying, "I have not yet been in a church that has a decent set of understandings of how to deal with differences when they arise." When we see the tremendous pain that unhealthy and unbiblical conflict can cause, and the tremendous long-term damage it can do to a church (note the previous section), I think it is extremely important that every congregation have some training in conflict resolution so that they have protection the next time a potentially divisive individual or issue enters the congregation.

I would like to recommend that every pastor read one pamphlet and two books in the area of conflict resolution: (1) Speed Leas, "How to Deal Constructively With Clergy /Lay Conflict," (2) Speed Leas, *Moving Your Church Through Conflict* (both are available from Alban; 1-800-457-2674), and (3) Kenneth Haugk, *Antagonists in the Church* (Augsburg Publishing House).

Antagonists in the Church is excellent in developing a response to a single individual who has a history of divisiveness. Haugk shows how much damage one such individual can cause a church. He discusses strategies that the church leaders and members can take early to reduce the damage done by such a person.

Leas's pamphlet and book describe in detail what happens when a group of people start to become divisive about an issue. He makes the wise point that one needs different approaches depending on whether a group is operating at Level 2 or Level 4. He suggests that different members in a congregation may be at different levels (for example, some might be at Level 1 while others are at Level 3). He describes methods appropriate to each level. I have not summarized all aspects of his two works in this chapter. I believe every pastor will be amply rewarded if he invests a few hours reading Leas's works.

From them a pastor can develop his own model for resolving church conflict. I believe that at least the lay leadership, if not the entire congregation, should be taught a model of conflict resolution. In the concluding pages of this book I will suggest one such model. Some of these steps are more philosophical, others more behavioral.

Practical Steps to Deal with Congregational Conflict

1. Differentness is not bad. We grow from receiving feedback from those who are different from ourselves.

2. We stop growing when we stop being willing to hear feedback.

3. When we cease being open to others, we lay the groundwork for conflict with those from whom we have closed ourselves off.

4. Give ourselves permission to feel what we are feeling. Sometimes Christians have suppressed their awareness of things that are bothering them, believing that such feelings are unchristian. A habit of chronic suppression of frustrations eventually harms everyone.

5. Identify *specifically* about what is bothering you. The examples below show the difference between being general and being specific.

General: "I don't think you really care about me"; *Specific:* "When you're counseling me in your office and you keep glancing at telephone messages on your desk, I feel like you're impatient with me to be finished so that you can get to your other work."

General: "I don't like the way you preach!"; *Specific:* "When you publicly make fun of a theological position that you know I hold, I feel belittled and angry."

6. Once you know specifically what is bothering you, decide whether it is important enough to share with the other person. If it will cause you to withdraw gradually from the other person out of hurt or anger, it is important enough to share.

7. If it is important enough to share, go directly to the other person and discuss it. Going to someone other than the person involved is gossiping. The whole church should be trained that if someone gossips to them, they should encourage that person to go directly to the other person involved. They then should follow up with the person to see whether he went to the other individual.

8. Concerning your pastor's leadership, distinguish between what are your preferences for how a pastor should function and what are those things identified in Scripture or in your pastor's job description. It's impossible for a pastor to suit every congregational member's preferences, and it's unreasonable for us to expect him to do so. If the problem is based on one of our preferences, our pastor doesn't feel led to move in the direction of our preference, and that preference is so important that we can't support our pastor's ministry because of its lack, *we* probably should leave and find a pastor who does meet our expectations.

9. State your issue and the *feelings* you have because of the issue to the other person. People are more likely to be willing to change if they hear your feelings about the issue.

10. Listen to the other person's side. By hearing the rationale, you may change your mind.

11. If both of you still have differences, see if there is a workable compromise that you could develop.

12. If the person (or pastor) is utterly unwilling to hear you and the issue is one of significance for the whole church, take one or two others with you and try again.

13. If the person still won't hear you and the issue merits this level of attention, take it to the appropriate board or committee.

14. The board or committee should assess whether this issue is significant enough to merit its action or whether it is primarily an individual issue that the person needs to resolve by making some personal adjustments or by finding another church more consistent with his expectations.

15. If the board believes that the issue is significant and that one or both parties need to make changes, it should specify the changes and meet with the two individuals to ask for their concurrence.

16. If one or both people are unwilling to abide by the suggested changes, the board or committee can make stipulations regarding both persons' responses so that the issue does not grow beyond these two people and cause wider disruption in the church.

17. If the issue is significant and relates to the pastor's leadership, the board and pastor should discuss the issue and see if a workable solution can be found.

18. If the pastor is unwilling to change because he believes that most of the congregation support his present positions and leadership style, the board can, with the pastor's knowledge, develop a means of polling the congregation. The method should be reviewed by everyone involved to ensure that there are no leading questions or that the wording or method would not damage the pastor's ability to function in a pastoral role after the poll is completed.

19. If the poll shows that most of the congregation support the pastor's present position or leadership method, the matter should be dropped (unless it relates to matters of morality or doctrinal orthodoxy).

20. If a poll shows that this is a significant issue for the congregation and that it is negatively affecting most of the congregation, the board can again ask the pastor to make a change. If he is unwilling, the board can inform the regional denominational executive of the problem. The executive can attempt to help the two sides come to an agreement.

21. If the pastor is still unwilling to change, the board should write out the specific changes they and the congregation are asking for, a statement of their willingness to work with the pastor in helping him make those changes, and the consequences if he will not.

22. If the pastor is willing to make changes, one or more of the following experiences could be encouraged:

A. Further education.

B. Personal counseling.

C. Monthly meeting with a small group from the board or congregation with whom the pastor is comfortable. This group would give him suggestions related to the issue of concern and provide regular feedback on how they see him progressing in that area.

D. Rest and recovery (useful in cases of burnout).

23. If the pastor is unwilling to make changes, the board may ask for his resignation. They should develop a fair severance package (it is appropriate for churches, like other organizations who employ professionals, to provide between 100 and 150 days of salary and benefits following separation).

My hope is that the earlier chapters of this book will help you choose a pastor whose abilities and interests complement your needs as a church, who would have a desire and flexibility to meet your expressed needs so that you never have to use the latter steps of this model.

May God bless and guide you as you choose your next pastor!

NOTES

Chapter 1

1. Loren B. Mead, *Critical Moment of Ministry: A Change of Pastors* (Washington, D.C.: Alban Institute, 1986), 72.

Chapter 2

1. C. Peter Wagner, *Leading Your Church to Growth: The Secret of Pastor/People Partnership in Dynamic Church Growth* (Ventura, Calif.: Regal, 1984).

Chapter 3

1. Mead, 21.
2. "On Calling a Pastor: A Manual for the Pastor Nominating Committee" (Atlanta: Presbyterian Church [U.S.A.], n.d.), no page numbers in booklet.
3. Mead, 20.
4. J. William Harbin, *After the Pastor Leaves . . . When Another Comes* (Nashville: Broadman, 1988), 5.
5. Several of the above points are from Harbin, 15–19.
6. Elisabeth Kübler-Ross, *On Death and Dying* (New York: Macmillan, 1969).
7. Mead, 41.
8. Mead, 39–40.
9. Mead, 40.
10. Lyle E. Schaller, *The Pastor and the People* (Nashville: Abingdon, 1973), cited in Robert W. Dingman, *The Complete Search Committee Guidebook* (Ventura, Calif.: Regal, 1989), 95.
11. Keith Reeve has written an excellent short article titled "While You're Saying Goodbye: A Checklist of Items for a Pastor's Consideration on Leaving a Congregation." This article can be found in the book *Saying Goodbye: A Time of Growth for Congregations and Pastors,* edited by Edward White (Washington, D.C.: Alban Institute, 1990), 112–14.
12. Bunty Ketcham, *So You're on the Search Committee* (Washington, D.C.: Alban Institute, 1985), 10.
13. Wm. Bud Phillips, *Pastoral Transitions: From Endings to New Beginnings* (Washington, D.C.: Alban Institute, 1988), 8–10.

14. Two liturgies for saying good-bye are included in the book *Saying Goodbye*, edited by White, 70–76.

15. Adapted from Phillips, 27–29.

16. White, *Saying Goodbye*.

17. Adapted from "Leaving the Pastorate: Staying in Town" by Rod Reinecke, in *Saying Goodbye*, edited by White, 103–104.

18. Richard J. Kirk, *On the Calling and Care of Pastors* (Washington D.C.: Alban Institute, 1973), 6.

19. These advantages are compiled from Leonard Hill, *Your Work on the Pulpit Committee* (Nashville: Broadman, 1970), 22–23 and Harbin, 11.

20. Mead, 55.

21. Church consultant Bunty Ketcham has said, "The success or failure of this new bond [between a church and a new pastor] is affected by many other factors besides the actual selection of a successor. When we look at failures, we find that some were affected by the state of the church well before the search process began. Perhaps a congregation did not attend to the grieving process. . . . Perhaps deep-seated conflict in the parish has gone unattended for years and therefore inundates and immobilizes a new pastor (*So You're on the Search Committee*, 3).

22. The following three ideas are adapted from an article by Duane Visser called "Firing Pastors Is Problem for Baptists" found in *The Chaplain's Newsletter* (Grand Rapids: Pine Rest Christian Hospital, 1990), vol. 21, no. 2, pp. 4–5.

23. John C. Fletcher, *Religious Authenticity in the Clergy* (Washington, D.C.: Alban Institute, 1975), cited in Mead, 32.

24. Thomas N. Gilmore, *Making a Leadership Change: How Organizations and Leaders Can Handle Leadership Transitions Successfully* (San Francisco: Jossey-Bass, 1988), 12.

25. Gilmore, 7–8.

26. Dingman, 32.

27. Hill, 24–25.

28. Hill, 19.

Chapter 4

1. Robert T. Mager, *Goal Analysis* (Belmont, Calif.: Lear Siegler/Fearon Publishers, 1972), v–vi.

2. Dingman, 120.

3. Elliot Brack, "Viewpoints: Modern Methods Often Ignored in Minister Selections," *Gwinnett Daily News*, June 15, 1986, 3C.

4. Mead, 2–3.

5. Taken with slight adaptation from Jean Shaw, "A Case of Unprofessional Conduct," *Eternity*, February 1980, 35.

6. Several of these groupings come from an article by D. G. Stewart, "Bishop (Elder)," in *The Zondervan Pictoral Encyclopedia of the Bible*, edited by Merrill D. Tenney (Grand Rapids: Zondervan, 1975), 1: 619. The exegetical comments within each category are from the commentators so designated within the discussion.

7. Donald Guthrie, *Tyndale New Testament Commentaries*, (Grand Rapids: Eerdmans, 1972), 14:80.

8. N. J. D. White, *The Expositor's Greek Testament* (Grand Rapids: Eerdmans, 1979), 4:111.

9. D. Edmond Hiebert, *The Expositor's Bible Commentary* (Grand Rapids: Zondervan, 1978), 11:430.

10. Hiebert, 431.

11. Guthrie, 82.

12. A. T. Robertson, *Word Pictures in the New Testament* (Nashville: Broadman, 1931), 4:572.

13. Hiebert, 431.

14. Hiebert, 431.

15. E. K. Simpson, *The Pastoral Epistles* (Grand Rapids: Eerdmans, 1953), 51.

16. Hiebert, 431.

17. Simpson, 51.

18. Robertson, 572.

19. Ralph Earle, *The Expositor's Bible Commentary* (Grand Rapids: Zondervan, 1978), 11:364.

20. Hiebert, 430.

21. Earle, 364.

22. Robertson, 572.

23. White, 112.

24. W. E. Vine, *An Expository Dictionary of New Testament Words* (Westwood, N.J.: Revell, 1940), 51.

25. Peter Drucker, "Drucker on Leadership," *Reflections from the Lamp* (Winter 1984), 3:1.

26. David Bradford and Allan Cohen, *Managing for Excellence: A Guide to Developing High Performance in Contemporary Organizations* (New York: Wiley & Sons, 1984), 62–63.

27. J. Donald Walters, *The Art of Supportive Leadership: A Practical Handbook for People in Positions of Responsibility* (Nevada City, Calif.: Crystal Clarity Publishers, 1987), 27–28, 51.

28. Walters, 56–57.

29. Many concepts in the paragraphs related to the five-step process of leadership are adapted from John P. Kotter, *The Leadership Factor* (New York: Free Press, 1988), 19–29.

30. Kotter, 29.

31. Walters, 11.

32. Walters, 22.

33. Fred A. Manske, Jr., *Secrets of Effective Leadership: A Practical Guide to Success* (Germantown, Tenn.: Leadership Education and Development, Inc., 1987).

34. Other examples of self-study formats can be obtained. One is *The Manual for Pastor-Parish Relations Committees,* published by the Center for Parish Development, 1448 Fifty-third Street, Chicago, Illinois 60615. Another is *The Guide for Congregational Self-Evaluation,* available from the Episcopal Church Center, 815 Second Avenue, New York, New York 10017.

35. Many of the items included in this general description are adapted from the *Church Profile Form* of the Reformed Church of America, 475 Riverside Drive, Room 1808, New York, New York 10155.

36. Dingman, 158.

37. Dingman, 158–59.

Chapter 5

1. Reprinted from *Eternity,* September 1980, 65.

2. Fred Smith, "A Holy Boldness Toward Money, and a Fear of Its Power," *Leadership,* Spring 1981, 51.

3. The comments on 1 Timothy 5:17–18 and Galatians 6:6 are adapted from an article by Wayne Grudem, "Don't Muzzle the Ox with Chicken Feed," *Eternity,* September 1980, 63–64.

4. Manfred Holck, "Pastors' Pay: Who Sets It and How?" *Leadership,* Winter 1980, 40.

5. Holck, 41.

6. Lyle Schaller, "The Changing Focus of Church Finances," *Leadership,* Spring 1981, 15.

7. Schaller, 13.

8. Holck, 44.

9. Paul Robbins, "Clergy Compensation: A Survey of Leadership Readers," *Leadership,* Spring 1981, 34–45.

10. Some of Mr. Sedrel's other writings include "How to Obtain or Make Current 'Median Family Income' Estates," "Comprehensive Pastors Salary Guide," "A Tax Savings That Most Pastors Overlook," and "The Pastor's Time." Points 1 through 6 come from Mr. Sedrel's writings.

11. Some readers may wonder about using the Median Household Effec-

tive Buying Income on two counts. First, the MHEBI is based on after-tax dollars; using this figure as a basis for the pastor's pretax income will underestimate what his salary should be. Second, the MHEBI is an estimate of family income; many women work and this factor affects the MHEBI, which could overestimate what the pastor should be paid. Trying to get exact figures in these two instances would make calculations exceedingly complex. To simplify matters, the assumption is being made (since most pastors' wives who do work only do so part-time) that these two factors roughly cancel each other out.

12. Harold Sedrel, "The Pastor's Time," unpublished paper, 1973.

13. Roy M. Oswald, *New Beginnings: A Pastorate Start Up Workbook* (Washington, D.C.: Alban Institute, 1989), 21.

Chapter 6

1. Gerald Gillaspie, "Finding the Right Pastor," *Voices,* Winter 1982, published by Trinity Evangelical Divinity School, Deerfield, Illinois.

2. Gilmore, 55.

3. Dingman, 51–52.

4. Gilmore, 62.

Chapter 7

1. Harbin, 20–21.

2. Dingman, 85–86.

3. A number of the ideas in the following sections were adapted from Harbin, 20–31, and Hill, 26–30.

4. Many of the following questions are taken from or adapted from an unpublished paper by Rev. Dennis Lacy entitled "Questionnaire for the Pastoral Candidate."

Chapter 8

1. Hill, 41–42.

2. Gilmore, 72.

3. Adapted from Harbin, 40–41.

4. Hill, 47–52.

5. Gilmore, 76.

6. These questions are taken from or adapted from questions found in Harbin, 51–52; Hill, 45–46; questions developed by the Reformed Church of America; questions developed by the Baptist General Conference; Gilmore, 80.

7. Gillaspie, 8.
8. Hill, 60.
9. Gillaspie, 8.

Chapter 9

1. Phillips, 66–67.
2. Oswald, *New Beginnings*, v.
3. Oswald, *New Beginnings*, 3.
4. Phillips, 57.
5. Roy M. Oswald, *The Pastor as Newcomer* (Washington, D.C.: Alban Institute, 1977), 4.
6. Dingman, 196–97.
7. Dingman, 200.
8. Anthony Plathe, "The Pastor Says Goodbye: How to Move through Good Friday to Easter," in *Saying Goodbye*, edited by White, 49–55.
9. Oswald, *New Beginnings*, 1.
10. Mead, 31.
11. Plathe, 55.
12. Plathe, 55.
13. Gilmore, 130.
14. Oswald, *New Beginnings*, 28–29.
15. Oswald, *Pastor as Newcomer*, 4–5.
16. This process was designed by Management Design, Inc., 8250 Winton Road, Cincinnati, Ohio 45231. It is contained in *Strengthening the Local Church Workbook*, United Church of Christ, 297 Park Avenue South, New York, New York 10010. The description in this chapter was based on a discussion by Oswald in *New Beginnings*, 31–32.
17. Phillips, 21.
18. Phillips, 59–63.
19. Cliff Stabler, "The Care and Feeding of Shepherds," reprinted from *Christianity Today* with permission.

Chapter 10

1. Speed Leas, *Moving Your Church Through Conflict* (Washington, D.C.: Alban Institute, 1985), 12.
2. John Esau, "How Long Should a Pastor Stay?" in *Saying Goodbye* edited by White, 15.
3. A. O. Hirschman, *Exit, Voice, and Loyalty: Responses to Decline in Firms, Organizations and States* (Cambridge, Mass.: Harvard University Press, 1970).

4. Ideas in this section are from Speed Leas, "How to Deal Constructively with Clergy/Lay Conflict" (Washington, D.C.: Alban Institute, n.d.), 5–7, and *Moving Your Church Through Conflict*, 1985), 13–15.

5. Oswald, *The Pastor as Newcomer,* 9.

6. Warner White, "Should I Leave? A Letter from One Priest to Another," in *Saying Goodbye,* edited by White, 3–14.

7. The following discussion is from a monograph, "How to Deal Constructively with Clergy/Lay Conflict," written by Speed Leas to summarize the results of the study.

8. Malcolm Leary, "Handling Conflict: Dealing with Differences—Creatively and Constructively." booklet published by the Association of Teachers of Management.

9. Leas, *Moving Your Church Through Conflict,* 19–22.

10. Frederic W. Farrar, *History of Interpretation* (Grand Rapids: Baker, 1961), 363–64.

11. Leas, "How to Deal Constructively with Clergy/Lay Conflict," 18.

APPENDIX A

Twenty-One Common Mistakes
Pulpit Committees Make

1.
Mistake: Failure to carefully select members of a PNC.
Results: May fail to represent important subgroups of the church (e.g., women and older members). PNC may end up including members who monopolize time and try to force decisions based on their views. There may not be enough new viewpoints represented so that the PNC makes decisions with the present and the future in mind. Unwise choice of committee members may result in factions developing on the PNC and later in the church. Potential candidates may be scared away from considering the church because of outspoken, dogmatic, or divisive PNC members.
Solution: Be careful in selecting members of this committee. See suggested criteria in chapter 2.

2.
Mistake: Too large or too small a PNC.
Results: Too small results in too much work per member or in failure to represent adequately all the important subgroups within a church. Too large means that discussions and decisionmaking take longer than necessary.
Solution: Appoint or elect between five and thirteen people, depending on size of congregation, whether a separate task force will do the self-study, and the number of applicants the committee will consider.

3.
Mistake: Failure to do self-study.
Results: PNC may not consider how the congregation, the new pastor, and the community will fit together. They may fail to consider the kind of person the congregation need who will challenge them to grow spiritually or to consider whether present programs need to be refocused. They may look for either a clone or an opposite of the last

pastor, depending on whether they liked him or not. They may fail to become specific about their expectations.

Solution: Do a careful self-study and submit it to some groups such as the judicatory and the board for their input. Then translate the results of the self-study into characteristics needed by the new pastor.

4.

Mistake: Failure to adopt an explicit code of confidentiality.

Results: Word can leak out about possible applicants. Such news that gets back to their present congregations can jeopardize their ministry there. If some of your own congregation members know of an applicant and like him, they can start campaigns within the congregation. Congregation members can resent it if some people have access to "inside information" about the candidates while they do not.

Solution: Develop an explicit code of confidentiality. PNC members should be prepared with sentences to use if someone tries to pry for confidential information (see chapter 2 for sample responses).

5.

Mistake: Failure to get a clear charge from the board.

Results: Can cause friction between the board and the PNC and the finance committee if the PNC does things without proper authorization. That can lead to failure to be reimbursed for PNC expenses or to early difficulties with the new pastor if the PNC promises things that the board later fails to uphold.

Solution: Get charter and charge in writing. Clarify any jurisdictional ambiguities early, again preferably in writing.

6.

Mistake: Failure to adequately use denominational resources.

Results: The PNC may use inefficient methods when better methods are available. Search process may take longer than necessary. The PNC may fail to become aware of candidates who would be excellent for the church. The PNC is much more likely to make mistakes if it does not consult with denominational leaders.

Solution: Use the search time to reestablish good connections and communication with judicatory.

7.
Mistake: Not clearly organizing the entire search process at the beginning.
Results: Committee members become confused, questions may not be asked of applicants in the most appropriate sequence, some applications may get "lost," and correspondence with applicants may become disorganized.
Solution: Plan all the steps in the process before taking any steps. Identify the most appropriate sequence for doing each part of the interview and selection process.

8.
Mistake: Allowing the interim to become an applicant.
Results: Serious problems may occur later if the congregation elects the interim, resulting in significant losses of church members and even church splits.
Solution: Make certain that the congregation, the PNC, and the potential interim know that the interim cannot be considered a candidate for the permanent position.

9.
Mistake: Having more than one PNC member communicate with applicants.
Results: Chaos. No one knows who said what to whom.
Solution: One person, usually the chair, is responsible for all formal communication with applicants.

10.
Mistake: Failure to be honest about congregational problems.
Results: Applicant may learn of problems through other sources. He may decide not to come because of lack of honesty or forthrightness of the PNC. If he does come, he may become quickly disillusioned for the same reason. He may not have the skills to handle the specific problem.
Solution: Be honest with applicants, especially finalists, about the problems in the church and let them decide if they can help the church resolve these problems.

11.
Mistake: Failure to prepare well for interviews.
Results: Awkward silences. Interviews may fail to accomplish

their intended purposes of obtaining and sharing vital information about the church and the applicant. PNC does not impress applicant, which affects his perception of the church.

Solution: Have clear goals for every interview. Each PNC member should know what questions to ask and in what order.

12.

Mistake: Failure to assess crossover candidates from other denominations with extra care.

Results: Applicant may have a history of immoral behavior, splitting churches, poor financial management, idiosyncratic theology, recurring power struggles, and so on that are a significant reason for wanting to leave his history behind him. Unless he has sought counseling and has shown that he has changed the traits that led to his problems in the other denomination, the same problems are likely to emerge in the new denomination.

Solution: Make certain to assess crossover candidates with extra care. Check with denominational overseers and members of previous two congregations (not his current church) to see if there are any problem patterns.

13.

Mistake: Failure to include consideration of the spouse and children in the recruitment process.

Results: May lose a good candidate through failure to consider adequately the needs of the spouse and children or through failure to allow the spouse to be part of the interview process. Also, may fail to detect that a candidate's partner may not be suited to a particular congregation or has personal problems that could significantly impair the candidate's ability to serve as pastor.

Solution: Focus on the needs of the entire family when preparing materials and conducting interviews. Include spouse in interviews.

14.

Mistake: Failure to be discreet when visiting another church.

Results: May cause unnecessary anxiety for the congregation of a pastor whom you may not even invite to be a candidate. If there is a faction against that pastor already, knowing that he is considering another church may intensify the activity.

Solution: Be sensitive if you visit a candidate in his home church.

Use your common sense to avoid drawing unnecessary attention to your visit. Despite your care, the ushers and a few members of the board probably will be aware of your presence, but the whole church doesn't have to know.

15.
Mistake: Overemphasizing pulpit skills.
Results: May select a pastor with impressive pulpit skills but with significant deficiencies in other areas.
Solution: Make certain that your selection process includes adequate emphasis on interpersonal skills, emotional healthiness, organizational skills, and other pastoral gifts.

16.
Mistake: Not scheduling enough time for the candidate and the congregation to meet each other.
Results: There may not be a good match on some other areas besides pulpit ability that are necessary for a good pastor-congregation relationship.
Solution: Schedule enough time and structure it so that the pastor, his family, and the congregation have an adequate opportunity to learn about each other and each other's expectations.

17.
Mistake: The "beauty pageant" approach.
Results: Demeaning to all candidates. You may lose some of your best candidates because they will be unwilling to participate in this type of selection process. Unfair to candidates seen first; congregation will be more likely to vote for those candidates seen most recently. Use of this approach has caused church splits.
Solution: Have PNC or board identify the candidate they believe is best for the church. Have church vote yes or no on him. Only if the congregation do not call him should a second candidate be presented to them.

18.
Mistake: Not keeping the interim pastor and associate staff informed.
Results: Poor staff morale, for they think the PNC or board does not consider them important. Poor morale can affect their perfor-

mance when the church needs them to give their best. May lose gifted associates during or after the interim because of their hurt and anger.

Solution: PNC gives associates and interim biweekly reports *before* reporting to congregation. One person (e.g., the vice-chair or secretary) can be designated to do this.

19.

Mistake: Not allowing enough grieving time between pastors.

Results: Congregation fails to or is slow to bond with new pastor. New pastor frequently compared with previous one, sometimes not objectively. Anger comes out at new pastor that is transferred from former pastor.

Solution: Design one or more experiences to facilitate grieving (e.g., the type of farewell reception suggested in chapter 3). If the former pastor was deeply loved or was at the church for ten or more years, purposely have an interim for a time before introducing any candidates for pastor.

20.

Mistake: Inadequate communication with candidates.

Results: Applicants feel anxious or angry at lack of information. Lack of feedback from numerous PNCs has caused some seminary graduates to be discouraged and give up plans for the ministry.

Solution: Have a well-organized plan of return letters, many of which can be form letters with minor changes for each individual. Keep applicants informed of the process and of their position in the process with the same regularity that you would desire if you were one of them.

21.

Mistake: Failure to get all agreements in writing.

Results: A verbal agreement is not passed on to the appropriate person or is misunderstood, or a board later disagrees with an agreement made by the PNC and fails to abide by it. The pastor or his family may become angry or disillusioned, which will affect his ministry at the church.

Solution: Get all agreements in writing. Agreements that have to be approved by someone other than the PNC should be so approved, with a notice of the approval in the appropriate board minutes.

APPENDIX B

Chart for Guiding the Board
and PNC During the Transition Process

(Tasks are roughly in sequential order. Read chart from left to right.)

Church Board Tasks

1. Pastor announces his resignation privately to board.

2. The board appoints a temporary chair of the PNC. Develops or revises charter and charge. Makes decision about size, composition, appointment or election, tasks, and authority. Contacts potential nominees confidentially to ascertain their willingness to serve. Discusses time commitment involved.

3. Pastor announces resignation to congregation. Temporary chair of PNC or chair of board addresses congregation.

4. Congregation or board selects the remainder of the PNC.

PNC Tasks

1. Temporary chair of PNC or chair of board addresses congregation. Will make biweekly reports to congregation starting now.

2. First meeting of PNC. Invite denominational representative. Go over recommended or required steps in the pastoral selection process.

Church Board Tasks

PNC Tasks

3. Second meeting. Share skills and feelings. Elect permanent chair, vice-chair, and secretary. Set weekly meeting time. Encourage PNC members to temporarily give up other church responsibilities.

4. Clarify any ambiguous wording in the charter or charge.

5. Identify procedural rules, e.g., confidentiality, etc.

6. Decide on a plan for the pastoral search. Develop your own procedures.

7. Conduct a self-study.

5. Help the congregation say good-bye to the departing pastor and his family.

8. Help the congregation say good-bye to the departing pastor and his family.

6. Decide whether the board or the PNC will be responsible for pulpit supply or interim. Delegate authority and responsibility accordingly.

9. If board delegates this responsibility to PNC, decide on pulpit supply or interim. Try out potential interims as pulpit supply first.

7. Board and PNC should decide whether there are psychological issues that need to be dealt with during the interim. If so, decide how to address them.

10. If during discussions or self-study the PNC concludes that there are psychological issues that need to be dealt with during the interim, discuss this with board.

Church Board Tasks

8. Whoever is responsible for interim should decide the nature and role of the interim pastor. Find him and empower him to fulfill that role.

9. Pastoral responsibilities need to be divided and delegated among board, associate staff, interim pastor, and congregational members.

10. Support the development of a worship program that keeps the congregation interested and involved. (This will be the most important way the board can be involved while the PNC is searching for and screening candidates.)

11. Decide the employment status of your associate staff and discuss this with them. Notify chair of PNC of the content of these discussions.

PNC Tasks

11. Whoever is responsible for interim should decide the nature and role of the interim pastor. Find him and empower him to fulfill that role.

12. Pastoral responsibilities need to be divided and delegated among board, associate staff, interim pastor, and congregational members.

13. Develop a pastor profile.

14. Ask for feedback on the self-study and pastor profile from judicatory and board.

15. Identify methods of finding potential applicants.

16. Develop introductory statements, questions, and written materials to use when communicating with referral sources.

17. Develop materials to send to potential applicants (description of church and Pastor's Information Form).

18. Send out materials.

19. Send a personalized form letter to everyone who

Church Board Tasks	PNC Tasks

sends in an application, describing the process.

20. Review initial applications. Do first round of eliminations. If you have many applications left, send nonacceptance letters to persons you have screened out.

21. Interview by telephone the *references* of the remaining candidates. Have three PNC members listen to applicants' sermons and independently rate. Do second round of eliminations based on these two factors. Reduce candidates to the top five or six.

22. Prepare for personal interviews. Identify questions, who will ask them, and in what order.

23. Have personal interviews with applicants and their spouses. Use group telephone interviews with those for whom distance prevents personal meetings.

24. Identify your strongest candidates. Visit them in their home church if you think that is necessary. Present candidate to board.

Church Board Tasks

PNC Tasks

25. With board and judicatory approval (if needed), schedule candidate and family to spend several days with you.

26. Have congregation vote on candidate. If vote is positive, extend a call. If vote is negative, recycle to Step 24.

27. Once you are certain the candidate is coming, send nonacceptance letters to remainder of applicants.

28. Send thank-you letters to those who have been helpful in your search process.

29. Destroy personal information of candidates that you have collected during the search process.

12. Thank the PNC for a job well done. If the church budget allows, send them and their spouses to a nice restaurant for a thank-you dinner. If it doesn't, find some other way to say "Thank you."

30. Celebrate!

31. Have at least one person (usually the chair) stay in touch with your new pastor to orchestrate practical help during his move and the first three months in his new position. Develop a transition team.

APPENDIX C

Example of a Charter and Charge to a PNC

Charter

The pastor nominating committee is a committee appointed by the church board when a present pastor announces his resignation. It will continue to exist until a new pastor has been called and has accepted that call and the committee is dismissed by the board. Persons appointed to the committee will be chosen based on their spiritual maturity, their knowledge of the needs of the church, their ability to work industriously and effectively as members of a team, and their ability to represent the church in a professional and Christlike way.

The committee's work will significantly affect the health and growth of the church for several years to come. It will require several hours each week for a period of three to eighteen months, occasionally longer. As a consequence no one will be appointed to the committee who is not aware of this time commitment and willing to make that commitment. It is hoped that committee members will be recompensed for their investment by knowing that their work is probably the most important work of any committee within the church. Committee members are encouraged to reduce other church-related responsibilities so that they have maximum time available for this work.

The committee will be composed of between five and twelve members, the exact number to be determined by the board depending on what they believe the optimal size for the committee will be at that time. The board will attempt to appoint committee members who represent the various needs and constituencies of the church. Between one-third and two-thirds of the committee will be members of the board.

Charge

The committee is empowered and authorized to do the following:
1. To engage in a self-study that identifies the needs, unmet

needs, opportunities for ministry, and vision for ministry our church can have in the next five years and beyond.

2. To develop a pastor profile based on Scripture's criteria for pastors found in 1 Timothy 3 and Titus 1, together with the qualities drawn from the self-study.

3. To develop methods for identifying pastoral candidates who meet those criteria and contacting those so identified.

4. To develop a method of screening candidates, which will enable the committee to evaluate each candidate on the basis of the pastor profile.

5. To eventually be able to recommend to the board one or more candidates it believes will meet the needs of our church and be able to identify specifically the reasons for the recommendation.

6. To keep the board, interim and associate staff, and congregation apprised of its work, without mentioning specific identities of candidates, on a biweekly basis.

7. To ask the church staff to provide secretarial support throughout the search process and to use church stationery and other supplies to accomplish its work. The committee may purchase needed materials not available at the church.

8. To arrange for printing of materials to be used in the search process. Costs should be approved by the board chair if they exceed the designated printing budget for the committee. That printing budget is $500.00.

9. To be reimbursed for mileage costs—when visiting applicants' churches or when an applicant comes for a personal interview—at the current estimated cost per mile provided by AAA. Food costs and lodging for applicants will be reimbursed, as will food costs for committee members when visiting candidates' churches. Overnight lodging by committee members needs prior authorization before being reimbursed. Requests for reimbursements should include receipts with accompanying explanation whenever possible.

10. To design ways of screening applicants that minimize costs to the church.

11. To be involved in salary and benefit negotiations with applicants within ranges specified by the board. The board must officially approve the final salary and benefit package.

12. To select an interim pastor and to offer him a salary designated by the board. A potential interim pastor should be used as a

supply pastor for at least two weeks before being offered an interim position. The interim contract should be for six months or until a permanent pastor is found, whichever comes first. It may be renewed if a permanent pastor is not available at the end of six months.

APPENDIX D

Congregational Self-Study Form

As part of our work in finding a new pastor, the pastor nominating committee would like your input in describing our church as you presently experience it. We would like your thoughts about its strengths, its weaknesses, the needs you foresee for our church in the next five to ten years, the priorities you think our next pastor should have, and the qualities you believe he should possess.

It will probably take from thirty to forty-five minutes to thoughtfully answer the questions on this questionnaire. Please consider this an investment in helping find the person who can effectively lead our church in the next phase of its growth. Try to be as honest as you can, even in your criticisms. Your questionnaire will remain anonymous unless you choose to sign it. Thank you in advance for your thoughtful input. It will be carefully reviewed by the committee.

Sex: Male____ Female____Age____ Number of Years Member or Attender____

Strengths

Please identify three or more areas in which you believe this church meets your needs or the needs of others well.

Weaknesses or Challenges

Please identify one or more areas in which you believe our church is not meeting your or other members' needs as well as it could.

Are there any unresolved problems within the congregation that you believe the board or the next pastor should attempt to address?

If your answer is yes, what are they? Please be as specific and complete as you can be.

Future Areas of Ministry

In what areas, if any, do you think our church should attempt to have a ministry in the next five to ten years that it is not having now?

In what areas of Christian living, if any, do you think you need to be challenged to grow by our next pastor?

Priorities

Pastors are called on to do many more things than their time allows them to do. As a consequence, they have to make decisions about priorities. In this process, it is helpful for them to know what their congregation view as priorities. Please look through the following list and circle the 1 beside the three or four activities you think are *most important* for your pastor to do. Go through the list a second time and circle the 4 beside those activities you believe are *least important* for your pastor to do (you may use 4 as many times as you wish). Circle either 2 or 3 (indicating moderate priority) beside the remaining activities.*

*Portions adapted from the Church Information Form of the Presbyterian Church (U.S.A.) and from Alvin Lindgren, *Foundations for Purposeful Church Administration* (Nashville: Abingdon, 1965).

Preparing for and leading corporate worship	1	2	3	4
Preparing for preaching and teaching	1	2	3	4
Congregational home visitation	1	2	3	4
Hospital and emergency visitation	1	2	3	4
Counseling	1	2	3	4
Training congregational members in and doing personal evangelism	1	2	3	4
Planning a balance of worship, teaching, and fellowship experiences for congregational members	1	2	3	4
Encouragement of international missions work	1	2	3	4
Involvement in missions to local community	1	2	3	4
Oversight of educational program of church	1	2	3	4
Administrative leadership of church staff	1	2	3	4
Ecumenical and interfaith activities	1	2	3	4
Involvement in regional denominational activities	1	2	3	4
Providing oversight for all activities and committees of the church	1	2	3	4
Providing oversight of building programs as needed	1	2	3	4
Encouraging the development of small groups to meet specific needs within the church	1	2	3	4
Dealing with people who might cause division	1	2	3	4
Monitoring and guiding church expenditures to stay within budget	1	2	3	4
Conducting weddings, baptisms, baby dedications, and funerals	1	2	3	4
Providing leadership when church discipline is needed	1	2	3	4

Controversial Issues

Christians disagree about a number of issues related to pastoral selection. We would like your thoughts on the following:

Would you be willing to consider a woman as your senior pastor? Yes____ No____ Perhaps____ Reason or comment_____

_____

_____

Would you be willing to consider a person for pastor who had at some time in the pastoral experience been involved in moral failure if there was evidence of genuine repentance since that time? Yes____ No____ Perhaps____ Reason or comment_____

Would you be willing to consider a person for pastor who has been divorced? Yes____ No____ Perhaps____ Reason or comment____

Qualities Our Next Pastor Should Have

Based on your knowledge of our church, of its present strengths and weaknesses, and of the needs we may have in the next five to ten years, please identify the qualities that you think are important for our next pastor to have. For example:

- ability to speak both English and Spanish and a knowledge of North American and Hispanic cultures
- someone with a distinct gift in personal evangelism, who can also teach others how to do it

Thank you for your time and input. Your responses will be considered carefully by the pastor nominating committee.

APPENDIX E

Sample Pastor's Information Form

This form will be copied so that it may be read by various members of the pastor nominating committee. To ensure legibility of the copies, please type or write clearly using black ink. None of this information will go beyond the committee without your permission.

Please attach a recent photograph of yourself if one is available

Personal and Family Information

Name in full _____

Address where correspondence should be sent

_____

Street address

_____

_____ ( ) _____

City   State   Zip   Phone   Office   Home

Do you wish the fact of your application to be kept confidential? Yes No

Date of birth _____ Married _____ Date of marriage _____

If you have children, please list their names and ages:

_____ _____ _____ _____

_____ _____ _____ _____

Have you or your spouse ever been divorced? _____ If yes, please explain. Use extra space if you wish. _____

_____

_____

_____

_____

_____

College and Seminary Education

School*	City and State	Degree	Major	Date Degree Received

*Please have each college or seminary send a transcript directly to us.

Are you licensed within our denomination? _____ Date? _____

Are you ordained within our denomination? _____ Date? _____

Do you or anyone in your family have any physical or mental handicaps that might affect your pastoral ministry? _____ If yes, please explain and specify how you have been able to carry on your ministry. Use extra space if necessary. _____

_____

Have you ever been convicted of a felony or misdemeanor? Yes ____ No ____

If yes, please explain on a separate sheet of paper.

References

Please list the names of five people who know you well and would be willing to serve as references. One of these should be your present district superintendent or the district superintendent for the last church in which you served. A second should be someone who knows of your academic abilities. The other three should be people you have pastored. Please drop a note or call each of these people to let them know we may be contacting them in the next few months.

1. District Superintendent_____ (   ) _____

Name   Phone   Work   Home

2. Academic_____ (   ) _____

Name   Institution   Phone   Work   Home

3. _____ (   ) _____

Name   Relationship   Phone   Work   Home

4. _____ (   ) _____

Name   Relationship   Phone   Work   Home

5. _____ (   ) _____

Name   Relationship   Phone   Work   Home

Personal Christian Experience

Please identify and discuss those experiences that you view as having been especially important in the development of your own Christian faith and life. Use additional space if you desire.

Pastoral Experience

Please discuss your previous pastoral or Christian service experience. For each experience, discuss what your responsibilities were, how long you served, the most important contributions you believe you made, and your reasons for leaving. If you have had a long pastoral career, focus on your last two or three pastorates. Use additional sheets if you desire.

(Note to PNCs: Add other questions based on specific needs of your church.)

Thank you for your time in completing this Pastor's Information Form. In addition to this form, please send us two tapes of representative sermons you have preached in the past six months and sign the following release.

"I hereby give the pastor nominating committee of _____ Church permission to contact my references and to verify the information given in this application."

Date	Signature

APPENDIX F

Sample Telephone Interview Form

Applicant's Name _____

Recommender's Initials _____ (Name appears only on master list)

Interviewer's Name _____ Date of Interview _____

Recommender has known applicant for _____years _____months.

Has known applicant in following capacity _____

Knows applicant _____slightly, _____ moderately well, _____very well.

In comparison to other ministers in his denomination, have recommender indicate Exceptional (5), Above Average (4), Average (3), Below Average (2), Serious Deficiency (1), Do Not Know (0). Circle recommender's answers.

1. Preaching ability	0	1	2	3	4	5
2. Worship-leading ability	0	1	2	3	4	5
3. Teaching ability	0	1	2	3	4	5
4. Ability to develop a vision for a church	0	1	2	3	4	5
5. Ability to communicate that vision to congregation so that it becomes theirs also	0	1	2	3	4	5
6. Ability to motivate others in healthy ways	0	1	2	3	4	5
7. Ability to translate vision into concrete plans	0	1	2	3	4	5
8. Ability as a church administrator	0	1	2	3	4	5

Specific strengths? _____

Specific weaknesses? _____

9. Ability to encourage others to develop their gifts	0	1	2	3	4	5

10. Earns loyalty of staff and congregation	0	1	2	3	4	5
11. Cares deeply about congregation	0	1	2	3	4	5
12. Is available and visible to staff and congregation	0	1	2	3	4	5
13. Works comfortably with church board and denominational officials	0	1	2	3	4	5
14. Can supervise others effectively	0	1	2	3	4	5
15. Gentleness	0	1	2	3	4	5
16. Dignified, good self-control	0	1	2	3	4	5
17. Hospitable	0	1	2	3	4	5
18. Ability to work without supervision	0	1	2	3	4	5
19. Open-mindedness, tolerance for reasonable differences of opinion	0	1	2	3	4	5
20. Capacity for objective evaluation of his own strengths and weaknesses	0	1	2	3	4	5

Problem Areas

Do you know of any problems in the following areas? (If yes, interviewer should include details on a separate sheet of paper.)

1. Unfaithfulness or any questionable behavior with opposite sex? Unhappy marriage for either partner?
2. Failure to discipline children?
3. Difficulty handling anger or frustration?
4. Any evidence of alcohol or drug abuse by pastor or spouse?
5. Failure of self-discipline in any area that significantly hinders role as pastor?
6. Spending beyond one's means in either personal or church situations?

7. Low energy level?

8. Anxious, fearful?

9. Dependent?

10. Low self-esteem? Unusual need for approval?

11. Manipulative?

12. Hostile, angry?

13. Tends to get into power struggles?

14. Shy, overly sensitive to criticism?

15. Pushy, aggressive?

16. Impulsive, hasty?

17. Is there anything else in this person's history or personality that might affect his ability to pastor?

18. Please indicate the strength of your overall endorsement of this person for pastor: __highly recommend, __recommend, __recommend with some reservations, __do not recommend.

Reference feedback for the first half of this interview can be quantified in the following way. Add up all the numerical ratings. Divide by 20 minus the number of items that the reference marked zero. The result will be the average score. The higher the average is, the more positive it is.

If the applicant has a significant problem in any area listed in the second half of the interview, and if this is confirmed by other sources, you may decide to disqualify the candidate no matter how good his score on the first part of the interview.

APPENDIX G

Criteria for Evaluating a Sermon

Use the following scale, comparing this sermon with the average sermon you are used to hearing in a local church (not on television). Use 5 for excellent, 4 for above average, 3 for average, 2 for below average, and 1 for seriously deficient. Compute average at bottom of page.   *Rating*

1. *Introduction:* captured my attention and interest. Made me want to hear the rest of the sermon.   _____

2. *Use of Scripture:* used Scripture to make, clarify, and illuminate points. Seemed to be used in context.   _____

3. *Logical continuity:* points of the sermon logically built on and followed one another.   _____

4. *Clarity:* the points of the sermon were clear.   _____

5. *Relevance:* the sermon topic was developed in a way that made me see the relevance for myself today.   _____

6. *Use of humor:* humor, if used, was appropriate to the setting and points of the sermon.   _____

7. *Use of self-disclosure:* if speaker used himself as an illustration, it helped make the sermon more meaningful.   _____

8. *Use of vocal inflection:* added appropriate emphasis and interest to the sermon. Did not scream or scold audience.   _____

9. *Use of illustrations:* were used to clarify or deepen the impact of a point but not to prove points.   _____

10. *Interest level:* I wanted to hear more sermons from this pastor._____

Total   _____
Average (total ÷ 10)   _____

APPENDIX H

Sample Letters

Sample Letter: To Potential Applicant
Whose Name Has Been Given By A Source

Date

Dear _____ :

Our church is in the process of searching for a new pastor. You have been highly recommended to us by _____.
We have enclosed a brief description of our church and its present ministries. If after reading this description you feel that your gifts and interests complement the needs we have as a congregation, we would encourage you to complete the enclosed Pastor's Information Form. If you have a resume prepared, we would be glad to receive that also, but we ask that you complete the enclosed form so that we have equivalent information from everyone.

Sincerely yours,

Chair

Pastor Nominating Committee

Sample Letter: Response to Resume Sent By Pastor Who Heard of the Opening

Date

Dear _____:

Thank you for submitting your resume. We are searching for a new pastor and appreciate your interest in letting us know of your availability and pastoral experience.

In order to have similar information on all pastors who are applying, we are asking each one to complete the enclosed Pastor's Information Form. We are enclosing a summary of our self-study so that you can more fully evaluate whether we are the kind of church whose needs match the gifts you perceive yourself as possessing. If they do, we encourage you to complete the enclosed application and send it to us as soon as possible.

Sincerely yours,

Chair

Pastor Nominating Committee

Sample Letter: Incomplete Application

Date

Dear _____:

Thank you for completing your Pastor's Information Form. In order for your application to be complete, we still need:

( ) Official copies of transcripts from college and graduate school work

( ) Two audiotapes of sermons you have preached in the last six months

We will let you know as soon as we have received them.

Sincerely yours,

Chair

Pastor Nominating Committee

Sample Letter: Application Complete

Date

Dear _____:

We have received your application, sermon tapes, and official transcripts. Your application is complete at this time. Because of the number of applications we have received, we expect that we will be spending the next few months talking with references, listening to sermon tapes, and reviewing what you have written. When that process is complete, we will schedule interviews with candidates we believe best meet the needs of our church as we understand them.

You need do nothing more at this time. We will contact you if we would like to have a personal interview with you and your spouse or when we make a final decision. Thank you for your interest in our church. It is our hope that God will guide both you and us as we seek to serve Him.

Sincerely yours,

Chair
Pastor Nominating Committee

Sample Letter: Nonacceptance Letter

Date

Dear _____:

Thank you for your interest in our pastoral vacancy. We apologize for the length of time between your application and our response to you. We have had many pastoral applicants with excellent training, experience, and commitment, and we as a committee have tried to carefully consider each applicant. Because we have only one pastoral vacancy, we have had to say no to many qualified applicants who are undoubtedly excellent pastors. We regret this and trust that God will continue to lead you into ministries that will be personally fulfilling and that will significantly strengthen His kingdom here on earth.

Sincerely yours,

Chair

Pastor Nominating Committee

Sample Letter: Thank You to Source or Reference

Date

Dear _____:

As you know, we have been searching for a new pastor for the past several months. God has rewarded our search, and we are looking forward to the ministry of _____, who will become our pastor on _____. We invite you to join us that day for a welcoming service. We also want to express our appreciation for the role you played in helping us find qualified candidates and assess their pastoral gifts. On behalf of the pastor nominating committee and our entire congregation, thank you.

Sincerely yours,

Chair

Pastor Nominating Committee

APPENDIX I

Process Summary Sheet*

Name of Applicant _____   Date

1. Pastor's Information Form received   _____
2. Initial verification letter sent   _____
3. Tapes received   _____
4. Transcripts received   _____
5. Second verification letter sent   _____
6. First elimination decision   _____
7. If definite "no," send nonacceptance letter   _____
8. Telephone references completed   _____
9. Sermon evaluations completed
       Committee member 1 (Initials)___ Score _____   _____
       Committee member 2 (Initials)___ Score _____   _____
       Committee member 3 (Initials)___ Score _____   _____
10. Second elimination decision   _____
11. Schedule of personal interview   _____
12. Decision based on personal interview   _____
13. Notification of decision sent   _____

*Suggestion: Staple this to the inside of the file folder for each candidate

GENERAL INDEX

SCRIPTURE INDEX

GLOSSARY OF
KEY TERMS

Alban Institute: a research and educational organization headquartered in Washington, D.C. It provides information, seminars, and consultation on various aspects of church growth, conflict resolution, and pastoral transitions.

appointive process: the process used by some denominations in which the judicatory appoints pastors to serve local congregations. Usually the local church or the local church's leadership has some opportunity to either affirm the appointment or ask the judicatory to reconsider the appointment. *Cf.* calling process.

Association: the judicatory for Southern Baptist churches in a specific geographical area. Has advisory function but no governing authority over local congregations.

autonomous churches: churches within those denominations that stress local church autonomy. Denominational judicatories have advisory function but no authority to intervene in local church matters. *Cf.* connectional churches

beauty pageant approach: a pastoral selection method in which the PNC presents several candidates to a congregation and has the congregation indicate its preference from among them. There is a consensus that this is not a wise selection method.

board: a generic name for the governing body of a local congregation.

calling process: the process used by denominations where local congregations choose their own pastors rather than having them appointed by some judicatory group or person. In connectional churches the denomination's judicatory must approve the call before it can be made. In autonomous churches this is not so.

canon: an assistant to an Episcopal bishop.

charge: an explicit statement from the church board authorizing the PNC to undertake certain activities in the search for a new pastor.

Church Information Form: a standardized form used by the Presbyterian Church (U.S.A.) for a congregation's self-study.

church profile: *see* self-study.

connectional churches: denominations in which local congregations are connected to and accountable to some higher denominational authority, such as a bishop or presbytery. *Cf.* autonomous churches.

crossover candidate: a pastoral candidate who formerly served in another denomination.

deacon board: the board in most nonconnectional (i.e., autonomous) churches.

developmental process: a process that normally occurs (or develops) over time. Such a process can occur within a group (such as the grieving process when a pastor leaves), or between a person and a group (such as the development of the relationship between a pastor and a congregation).

diocese: the governing body (judicatory) for Episcopal churches in a specific geographical area.

exit interview: an interview between a PNC and a departing pastor. Such meetings can allow both groups to share their feelings and understand the other's perspectives.

honeymoon period: a period immediately after a new pastor comes to a church in which there is a high level of harmony and affirmation.

interim consultant: a person with special training who helps a congregation objectively look at its history, identity, sense of mission, and expectations of its pastor. Also called vacancy consultant.

interim pastor: a person hired, when a church is between pastors, to perform many or all the duties normally done by a "permanent" pastor.

judicatory: a denomination's governing body or individual for a specific geographical area.

Letter of Understanding: a letter that provides a structure for the future relationship between a departing pastor and a congregation.

National Association of Church Business Administration: an organization headquartered in Fort Worth, Texas, that gathers and distributes information on salary and benefits for church workers. It also provides seminars and written materials on various aspects of church business administration.

oscillation: a process that sometimes occurs following a pastoral change, in which people within the congregation either reduce or increase their level of activity within the church.

overseer: someone who oversees many local congregations. Alternate names are bishop (United Methodist and Episcopal churches), state overseer (Church of God), state superintendent (Assemblies of God), district superintendent (Christian and Missionary Alliance), or district president (Lutheran church: Wisconsin synod).

parish committee: the governing board in a United Methodist church.

Pastor Profile: a specific description of the characteristics a PNC decides a new pastor should possess. A profile can be drawn from Scriptural criteria, congregational and judicatory input, and information from the self-study about the kind of leader needed to guide the church effectively for the next five to ten years.

Personal Information Form: a standardized form used by the Presbyterian Church (U.S.A.) that gives congregations information about pastors within the denomination.

PNC (Pastor Nominating Committee): the group designated for the responsibility of finding, screening, and recommending a candidate to the church board or congregation.

polity: a denomination's form of government.

presbytery: (1) the governing body (judicatory) for Presbyterian churches in a specific geographical area, or (2) all the Presbyterian churches, ministers, and members in a specific geographical area.

pulpit supply: a method used by some churches when they are between pastors where speakers are hired to preach one or two Sundays at a time but do not assume other pastoral duties. *Cf.* interim pastor.

rector: the pastor of an Episcopal church.

reference: someone who knows an applicant well and is willing to share that information with a PNC.

referral source: someone who is willing to recommend names of potential pastoral applicants to a PNC.

self-study: an in-depth examination, conducted by a church on itself, to look at its past, present, and future. It can be used to help parishioners personalize their mission, to acquaint pastoral applicants and candidates with the church, and to provide guidance in developing a Pastor Profile.

session: the governing board of a Presbyterian congregation.

unfinished business: the psychological phenomenon where people who have strong unexpressed feelings are unable to deal objectively and fairly with other tasks and people in their lives because the unexpressed feelings keep intruding into their present work and relationships.

vacancy consultant: *see* interim consultant.

vestry: the governing board of an Episcopal congregation.